Positive Psychology and Family Therapy

Positive Psychology and Family Therapy

Creative Techniques and Practical Tools for Guiding Change and Enhancing Growth

By

Collie Wyatt Conoley

and

Jane Close Conoley

WILEY

John Wiley & Sons, Inc.

Library of Congress Cataloging-in-Publication Data:

Conoley, Collie W. (Collie Wyatt), 1949-
    Positive psychology and family therapy: creative techniques and practical tools for guiding change
and enhancing growth/by Collie Wyatt Conoley, Jane Close Conoley.
        p. cm.
    Includes bibliographical references and index.
    ISBN 978-0-470-26277-1 (pbk.)
    1. Positive psychology. 2. Family psychotherapy. I. Conoley, Jane Close. II. Title.
    BF204.6.C67 2009
    616.89'156–dc22   2008047050

To M. Gilbert Conoley, my dad,
who taught me my first lesson in positive psychology.

Additionally:

In the early 1960s he created a Community Action Agency for two counties in Texas providing Head Start Centers, Family Planning Centers, Neighborhood, Youth, and Job Training Centers. In the late 1960s, he headed a multicultural team that desegregated the public schools of Texas. None of these movements were popular or easy, but he enjoyed them and he loved us.

Thanks, Dad.

Table of Contents

Foreword

A S THE REFERENCE section of this book attests, there is no shortage of extant family therapy books. A reasonable reader may wonder why we have decided to add to this already extensive library. While being explicit about the history of our subject matter, what we've learned from others and how the research and clinical expertise of our predecessors and contemporaries continue to influence us, we think we have something novel and important to share about helping families reach optimal levels of functioning. The evidence-based components of our approach are highlighted in the pages that follow. Of primary importance, however, is our assertion that therapeutic change in families depends on abandoning the pathology-oriented past of psychological interventions while embracing and expanding the reemerging science of positive psychology.

We have the advantage of having seen many, many families in therapeutic contexts and have had the opportunity to do research on families. We have also had the privilege of traveling around North America and to Asia, Africa, Europe, Australia, Central America, and the Middle East where we've been able to observe and interview families. We don't suggest any "universal" understandings of families, but we have tested our ideas and learned from many others over the past 32 years. In fact, anything of use in this book comes from our interpretation of what we've learned from others. Material deemed useless by readers (we hope a very small amount) is due only to our limited abilities to draw together the several fields of study that inform expert family therapy practice.

We have also had the great advantage of knowing many different forms of families. These have contained individuals of both sexes, all sexual orientations, some with a certified marriage arrangement, and others without the choice or opportunity for such formal arrangements. So we know families with one parent, two parents, and multiples parents, and families that flourish with biological, adopted, or fostered children. The challenges facing each of these forms differ in some ways, but the dynamics associated with building happiness among the members are surprisingly constant.

Of course, we are members of multiple families—our families of origin, our own nuclear family, and the new families being formed by our children and our siblings. The easiest view is not always gained by these up-close and personal experiences, but our reflections on our own families' lives have enriched and humbled us beyond description. Our parents gave us many wonderful experiences, insights, and privileges that we hope to share as generously as they were given. Our three children, Brian, Colleen, and Collin; their partners, Beth, Greg and Samantha; and our two grandchildren, Haley and Michael, continue to be sources of joy and amazement. Their lives fascinate, befuddle, and inspire us in our career goal to be facilitators of family success and happiness. They have not always enjoyed our somewhat relentless attention to family processes, we are sure, but they all have the grace and emotional intelligence to humor their parents and grandparents. Thank you.

Also, we thank our long-time friends and colleagues at several universities who have been willing to discuss and debate the meanings of mental health, psychotherapy, and family systems. That list is very long, but our family of friends from across the nation and world know who they are and have been true lights in our lives.

Our experiences with each other and with all the others in our lives have convinced us that happiness is the key human goal that must be pursued for optimal living. Happiness is not just the absence of sorrow. Happiness produces growth for individuals and families—and growth is what it's all about for families. Family therapists who orient their work in the direction of family happiness will offer an effective support for family development.

Collie Wyatt Conoley and Jane Close Conoley
October 2008

The Foundational Constructs of Positive Family Therapy

GOAL OF CHAPTER 1

Positive Family Therapy combines systems theory and positive psychology to derive an approach that builds upon the strengths of a family to enhance the growth of each individual member. We believe our approach has some unique aspects; however, the approach is based on research from many sources. This chapter presents the broader theory and empirical basis for Positive Family Therapy.

Family therapy has deep roots in viewing families as systems. Identifying Positive Family Therapy as systemic does not inform the sophisticated systems thinker. The information may be similar to saying we live in the western hemisphere when you ask for our address. Each family therapy theory focuses on the application of some systems concepts.

Similarly, saying our approach is based upon principles of positive psychology only begins the journey. The rich research and theories that historically anchor the current wave of positive psychology activity have taken many different routes from personality and social psychology. Carl Roger's and Abraham Maslow's Humanistic Psychotherapy unfolded very differently from Steve de Shazer and Insoo Kim Berg's Solution Focused Therapy, but each of these inform Positive Family Therapy. We are enriched by their foundational work in positive psychology embedded in psychotherapy. We also have the advantage of Martin Seligman, Sonja Lyubomirsky, Barbara Fredrickson, Shelly Gablel, Shane Lopez, Michael Scheel, and many more researchers and thinkers cited throughout this volume. While we cannot name all of those who deserve credit, we do want to thank our scholarly forebears and colleagues.

Like every field of study, family therapy has a language used by its scholars. The language has the advantages of precision and shared understanding for researchers. Such scholarly languages have the disadvantage, however, of making important constructs inaccessible to learners or novices from other fields (i.e., jargon). The following pages outline the key theoretical perspectives and research results that form the basis of techniques described in Positive Family Therapy. In subsequent sections, these constructs will be presented in everyday language so that practitioners will have assistance in translating complex and nuanced psychological realities to people who are not mental health experts but who need a working knowledge of how to improve their lives.

Key concepts: boundaries, causality, circularity, constructivism, ecology, equifinality, homeostasis, morphogenesis, morphostasis, permeability, physical science metaphors, positive psychology, recursive, similar proposition, social constructivism.

THE MAJOR CONSTRUCTS

SYSTEMS THEORY BASICS

Ludwig von Bertalanffy (1976) devised general systems theory as a universal theory that would allow understanding of all living systems. While, perhaps, not achieving the original intent, his general systems theory was used by scholars and practitioners in family therapy as a way to describe the relationships operating in families. Systems theory grew in application beyond mere biological systems to organizations of many different sizes and structures.

The definition of a *human system* is people in interaction by some similar proposition (von Bertalanffy, 1976). The key issues are the interactions and similar proposition. The term *similar proposition* means that the interaction among the people is somewhat predictable or governed by the norms of the system or family. When one person in the system acts, every other person is influenced, which again influences the person who initially acted, and so on and on. This is the *recursive* nature of living systems. Because the system is living and developing, a constant process of change is always in place, which is called *morphogenesis*. Yet the change remains small enough so the system remains intact, which is called *morphostasis* (Keeney, 1983). The mutual influence of systems describes the foundational contribution of the theory to family therapy. A system member can be helped or harmed by the system. Similarly, a system member can help or harm the system. Interaction happens continuously. Because a family system, however configured, is the most influential system in a person's life, facilitating the family's functioning helps each member. Each member is the family change agent who cares more about and is more consistently involved with the family than any family therapist.

The definition of a *family system* identifies a family as people in interaction by a similar proposition. A family system includes people who historically could be considered extended family, nuclear family, or non-related people who live together intimately. While we will often use examples that do not include larger family units or nonrelated units of people, these constellations are applicable. Family from our systemic definition is not culturally bound but is functionally defined. We wish to work with the system(s) that is/are most influential to the individual's or individuals' growth.

Positions in family systems relate to family role or family subsystems (e.g., parent, child, stepparent, parental child), age (e.g., birth order), temperament (e.g., tendencies to compromise versus to demand singular compliance), and to the family's history and culture. For example, in the U.S. majority culture we expect the father in a family to have greater influence than a child and older children to be more powerful than younger children. We also observe, however, that in many one-parent families or families with a large number of children, a child starts to take on the role of a parent because of the parent's need for support or help in raising other children. Family therapy welcomes different configurations of families and influence within families. We have worked with families that include grandparents, aunts, and friends who were imbued with great influence within the family.

We also see that family position can be influenced by the temperament of the individuals. Explosive and demanding parents or children may gain inordinate power in a family if the others are submissive to their tantrums or if the tantrums are extreme. Skill differences can play a role in family position if, for example, English speaking children become the translators or culture brokers for their non-English speaking parents. The child can accrue great influence within the family beyond that predicted by their ages or their heritage group.

The more influential subsystem of a family can be thought of as an executive system (preferably the adults). The executive subsystem can promote or mute change with greater power than the other systems. Understanding who belongs to the executive system and how well it functions is important. The executive system can contain a grandparent or religious leader who is not living with the family but may need to be included, even symbolically, in all important decisions.

If not every family member can attend therapy sessions, the members present can be asked to speak on their behalf (e.g., "If your father was here today, what would he say?"). Part of the executive subsystem is the memory of historical family members who communicated the family culture. Their contribution is important to respect. We particularly notice these influences when the family culture is very different from our own or when rapid acculturation is occurring or when immigration experiences have required parting with extended family.

Systems can be thought of as having boundaries (Minuchin, 1974). A *boundary* determines who is in a particular system/subsystem and who is outside. Systems within families or between families must interact. For example, the subsystem of children should be in communication with the parents. And the family should be in communication with the children's schools. Boundaries are constructs that allow us to describe the amount or quality of the interactions. These boundaries may be quite permeable, suggesting that, for example, information, affection, and supervision flow easily between parents and children.

Or the boundaries may be impermeable. Parents may keep secrets from each other or from their children. Or a parent may be distant or unapproachable to children, thus representing a disengaged or rigid boundary. Families that are pressured by illness or economic distress may withdraw from others as they attempt resolution and, thus, inadvertently be deprived of important resources. Some boundaries must exist for there to be an entity that can be defined as a family or a person. The most adaptive amount of boundary permeability is complex to estimate. The functionality is determined by the attributes of the individuals, their developmental tasks, and their culture. These metaphorical membranes influence the family system's resilience in the face of stress. For example, during a crisis these membranes may be too open or too closed. Family members can experience negative feelings because others seem too intrusive or too distant, resulting in an experience of being abandoned, exposed, or controlled.

Another essential prediction from systems theory is that the totality or whole of the system is more than the sum of the parts (von Bertalanffy, 1976). Knowing the individuals in the system does not tell us everything about the system's functioning. For example, well-meaning people can develop very poor relationships within families—an outcome that may not be readily predictable from knowing each person individually. Conversely (and more happily), troubled or troubling people can blossom and thrive in a facilitating system or family. A massive research tradition from social, community, and developmental psychology illustrates the power of the setting and group on the behavior of the individual, which gave gave rise to a school of ecological psychology (Bronfenbrenner, 1999). This theoretical and research tradition is closely related to systems thinking and explains the importance of developing healthy physical, social, emotional, and cognitive environments to support developing individuals. The ecological perspective also provides explanations for the long-lasting effects of trauma and deprivation on human development. Ecological approaches to physical and mental health goals are informed by general systems theory (Bronfenbrenner, 1999).

Equifinality.   This principle in systems theory emphasizes that there are many ways a final state can be reached by an open living system (von Bertalanffy, 1976). The final state could be a goal, signifying that there are many ways to reach a goal. By extension, there are many ways that we could arrive where we are today. The principle of equifinality has direct implications to psychotherapy. Understanding that there are an infinite number of ways for us to reach our goals opens up a great deal of flexibility and optimism. Alternately, people with the same problems or strengths can have very different early life experiences.

Recursive Interaction, Causality, and Change.   The interactional patterns of a family system are recursive rather than linear (Bateson, 1972; Becvar & Becvar, 2003). In this context, *linear interaction* implies the existence of a first and definite cause. Imagine kicking a rock. Knowing the force of the kick and the size of the rock will predict the outcome. In contrast to linear interactions, *recursive interaction* describes people's actions as reverberating reactions to other people, situations, memories, and perceptions. In such circular systems, certainty about causality is illusive. For example, instead of imagining kicking a rock, imagine kicking a person. Reactions to such an event are unpredictable. How was the kick interpreted? Was the kick initiated to kill a snake about to bite my leg? What prior relationship existed between the perpetrator and the victim? Speaking of initiation, what initiated the kick? What is the reaction to the reaction of the kick?

The range of consequences emanating from the kick and preconditions to the kick is vast. Possibilities vary from mumbled regrets, to dangerous brawls, to a teasing return kick, to a kiss. Recursive interactions among humans defy exact prediction. Only a known history of interactions and the prevailing *propositions* of the relationship give us limited predictive power. For example, do the older children in a family bully the younger one with impunity? Or are the older children held to higher standards of behavior because of their age and expected to bear the slings and arrows (or kicks) coming from their baby brothers and sisters? We need to know the propositions that bind the system to make an educated guess. The guess is always an incomplete description because it cannot include the beginning or the end, only a snapshot of the cycle of interactions. A better description contains more cycles of interactions but all description is incomplete.

Causality is a very popular idea for humans. Cause and effect is how we imagine the world works. We are drawn to figure out why things happen and tend to seek singular causes to events we witness or experience. Identifying causes and their effects is a basis of modern physical science. Physical science is the most powerful paradigm or metaphor we have to understand many of the mysteries of our universe. Close investigation of the most basic lawful behaviors and constituent elements is the path we equate with the scientific method. Psychotherapy has been influenced by the power of the physical science metaphor.[1] The link between psychotherapy and physical science can be traced back to psychotherapy's development in Europe and in the United States by physicians trained in the physical science model of causality. In the same way that particular germs, disease processes, or trauma events could be linked to human misery, certain historical or current psychological events or biological vulnerabilities could explain mental illness. Close ties between psychotherapy and medicine are also explained by the medicine's high status in the twentieth and twenty-first centuries. Although there are strong benefits associated with understanding humans as singular physical entities (i.e., we are not mind and body—just body), the predominance of the physical science metaphor has some unfortunate influence on the practice of psychotherapy.

A physical science metaphor misleads psychotherapists because the logic leads us to assume that human characteristics (e.g., values, desires, feelings, sense of self) are governed by the same causal principles of change associated with mechanical objects. Translating cause-and-effect reasoning to psychotherapy creates expectations of a straightforward causality. If the engine of a car does not start, the most important step is to identify the source of the problem. What critical part is failing? There is an identifiable cause. After an accurate assessment of the problem the dysfunctional part can be replaced. The car is functional once more! Simple cause-and-effect reasoning leads us to believe that understanding the cause leads inevitably

---

1. Often the historical metaphor of psychotherapy has been termed the medical model. We think that using the term *physical science* more clearly depicts the theoretical issues.

to a cure for the problem. In fact, the very useful psychological field of *functional behavior analysis* is closely modeled on this approach with specific strategies to identify presenting problems, their antecedents (i.e., causes), their consequences, and the contexts in which they appear (O'Neill, Horner, Albin, Storey, & Sprague, 1997). As useful as this approach can be in certain circumstances, it is not the most effective strategy to support positive change for whole families. The central concern of the approach is on problem behavior and the problem of an individual. Also, the perspective is typically linear in cause-and-effect reasoning.

A physical science metaphor relies on identical inputs always predicting identical outputs. While it is clearly true that installing the correct part in a car or using the right fuel predicts better performance, such certainty is rare with humans. For example, successful family routines such as shared dinner times or family vacations may become distasteful based only on the changing ages of the children. Almost every parent has had the experience of doing the same thing with a child and getting a very different reaction sometime between the ages of 11 and 16 years old. While many physical systems are best cared for by providing unchanging contexts (e.g., salinity of water, temperature ranges, titration of drugs), human systems have developmental trajectories, contexts, and moods that are quite complex to predict.

System theorists explain this complexity as exemplifying the many internal developmental and micro-, meso-, and macro-systemic variables that interact to produce every human behavior. Humans have a developmental trajectory in physical, cognitive, emotional, and social dimensions. As noted by the humanists of the last century, humans are driven to greater levels of complexity and more advanced forms of judgment across their life cycles. This internal development takes place in interaction with many other developing systems (e.g., other people, schools, work places, neighborhoods).

In addition to the sheer number of interactions that characterize family life, humans also create meaning from their experiences. They make interpretations about their own and others' behaviors. These vast networks of meaning interact as people make life choices. Perhaps more simply, philosophers and religious leaders point to human free will as a "wild card" in the process of predicting behavior. Cars do not make meaning and so they can be repaired based on presenting problems. People's behaviors challenge this assumption. Effective psychotherapy requires that our metaphor for human change/repair be more flexible. Basically, we must consider that positive human change can occur even when the "cause" is unknown. In fact, the "cause" may be irrelevant and relentless pursuit of root causes of family presenting problems may be harmful. If family interaction is recursive or circular, linear investigation strategies may be ineffective and become part of the problem. Beyond very simple reflexes, it is difficult to think of a human response that occurs every time a specific stimulus is presented (von Bertalanffy, 1976).

Structural Determinism. The determining factor of change in a system is the structure of the system. This is called *structural determinism* (Maturana, 1974). If a change attempt occurs in a manner that a family system cannot assimilate, the family does not change. For example, we may ask a parent to give his child a dollar every time the child cleans the kitchen. If, however, the parent believes that giving a dollar is bribing the child, the parent will not engage in the assigned intervention. A different system could have found the same intervention successful. The influence of the change is determined by the system not the intervention. We cannot blame the family because our interventions do not help them. Just as it is not reasonable for parents to blame each other for not behaving in accordance to the other's plan.

Therapeutic cooperation with structural determinism is achieved by selecting interventions that build on a family's strength. Helping a family grow by building upon strengths makes use of existing abilities and attitudes that are readily available for use in new areas of growth (de Shazer et al., 2007). Constructivism and social constructivism provide a critical perspective in understanding why the system or family determines what will be helpful.

Constructivism and Social Constructivism. Two other metaphors (models or theories), in contrast to physical science, provide some direction. These are constructivism and social constructivism. Focusing on the intrapersonal, *constructivism* describes the creation of meaning about the world occurring within each person's reasoning. From this perspective, an objective reality cannot be known; only a representation or subjective understanding created by our cognitive processes is available for shared discussion (Rudes & Guterman, 2007). Each of us creates our own reality based on our current perceptions interacting with our past experiences and our processing abilities.

Imagine the kick again. Upon being kicked, I could perceive that I am in a great deal of pain. Additionally, I could remember past experiences of being taunted by neighborhood bullies who enjoyed humiliating me by making me cry in public. And finally, my processing of the information could be influenced by my autonomic nervous system ramping up to a fight-or-flight response. With this snapshot of my internal processes, my reality of the kick becomes somewhat clear. Because of all the meaning associated with receiving the kick, you might understand my reacting with a bigger kick toward my constructed assailant.

Social constructivism, on the other hand, focuses on the interpersonal realm. *Social constructivism* describes knowledge existing through our interactions with each other, especially through language (Bruner, 2004; Gergen, 1985, 1997, 2000). Reality is cocreated through shared interactions. As we discuss issues, our beliefs about the issues emerge and congeal. We influence the reality of others and others, in turn, influence our reality. A negotiation of what is known or believed occurs during the conversations. Through our interactions with each other we discover our beliefs and others know us. The negotiation of reality makes recursive influence even more evident.

Another visit to the exemplar kick! Before you kick me, you shout, "Watch out for the snake crawling up your leg!" Then you kick me and exclaim, "Wow that was close!" If I enter into the construction built on your statements then my reaction is very different than before. Even if I never see the snake, I thank you for kicking me. Our interaction created another reality of the kick.

Constructivism and social constructivism are theories about how we create meaning—how we create reality. One very important creation is the self. How do I know who I am? Am I actually able to determine who I am? A basic contrasting question is, am I able to define myself or do my relationships define me? (Gergen, 2000; White & Epston, 1990). The definition of self highlights a difference between constructivism and social constructivism. A part of the psychological community has been moving toward the answer supplied by social constructivists: Self is a story that is created and recreated through stories (Bruner, 2004; Gergen, 2000). Internal and external conversations about our characteristics create who we are.

Shared conversations among people—who they are and what they believe—form cultures. Many things can influence these conversations—for example, prevailing religious convictions or historical developments. Social constructivists focus on the power of human interaction to create the realities in which people live (Gergen, 2000).

Therapists have observed that family conversations create the systems that describe problems and solutions (Anderson & Goolishian, 1988). The agreement and energy surrounding a problem as the topic can create a system that is organized around a particular definition of a problem. Perhaps when a family first enters therapy this is the structure. At least some powerful part of the family (and perhaps people outside the family as well) seems inflexibly engaged in conversation about a definition of "the problem." Often a major difficulty in family therapy involves moving the conversation from the problem to an ongoing conversation about the goal.

The perspectives provided by both constructivism and social constructivism offer important therapeutic wisdom. People surely have the power of internal and independent constructions of self and others based upon history, present perceptions, and personal abilities. In addition, it is equally obvious that people construct meaning based upon the stories they build with others or the stories they are mandated to accept. Both constructive processes are important in understanding reality and change. As subsequent chapters will illustrate, the ability to think using the technique of *both/and* reasoning as opposed to a singular reliance on *either/or* reasoning serves family therapists well. The reality of either/or reasoning requires a right and wrong perspective. Either my way is correct or your way is. Embracing both/and reasoning means that both can be helpful perspectives for growth and high functioning.

Two principles of communication should be continuously on our minds. The first one is that we cannot *not* communicate. The second is that communication can never be taken back (Stuart, 1980). By writing that we cannot *not* communicate, I mean that we are always communicating, even when we say nothing and twitch not a muscle. If a father sits quietly while the rest of the family is celebrating Marla's good grades, he is communicating. As newcomers to the family system we may not know what his noncelebratory behavior means, but the family knows that he is making a statement. If we suspect child abuse but do nothing, we are making a statement about the power of the perpetrator to bully even the therapist.

The principle that many people overlook is the axiom that communication cannot be taken back. "You really look awful in that sweater!" "Oh, I didn't mean it! I take it back." Once you think I do not like your sweater, the issue is clearly in front of us. This principle makes therapists work hard in family therapy. Allowing or encouraging angry, hurtful communication in a therapy session damages relationships further. Clients often view family therapy as an invitation to release all pent-up frustrations on another family member. Cruel communication harms relationships in session or out.

This concludes the systems theory presentation. Next we introduce positive psychology.

POSITIVE PSYCHOLOGY

"Positive psychology is the study of the conditions and processes that contribute to the flourishing or optimal functioning of people, groups, and institutions" (Gable & Haidt, 2005, p. 104). Helping families achieve conditions and processes that contribute to their optimal functioning or flourishing is an ideal addition to family therapy. Every family can embrace wanting to function optimally. The current research in positive psychology has given new vigor to the intersection of research in psychotherapy and optimal human functioning. Positive psychology research reveals how our ordinary strengths and virtues lead to functioning well psychologically (Sheldon & King, 2001).

> The field of positive psychology at the subjective level is about valued subjective experiences: well-being, contentment, and satisfaction (in the past); hope and optimism (for the future); and flow and happiness (in the present). At the individual level, it is about positive individual traits: the capacity for love and vocation, courage, interpersonal skill, aesthetic sensibility, perseverance, forgiveness, originality, future mindedness, spirituality, high talent, and wisdom. At the group level, it is about the civic virtues and the institutions that move individuals toward better citizenship: responsibility, nurturance, altruism, civility, moderation, tolerance, and work ethic (Seligman & Csikszentmihalyi, 2000, p. 5).

The study of positive psychology moves us even further away from a physical science metaphor for psychological intervention. Positive psychology clearly focuses psychotherapy outcomes beyond the goal of "no problem" or maintenance of a status quo. Mental health is not simply the lack of mental illness. Positive psychology investigates the paths that lead to happiness, fulfillment, and flourishing. These lofty goals provide a transformative understanding of psychotherapy that is particularly useful with families. Families are charged with facilitating each individual's capacity for love, vocation, sociability, forgiveness, and so on. Helping families know how to better perform their role as a system is an ideal fit for family therapy.

The critical research findings in positive psychology that translate directly to psychotherapy involve the importance of choosing a goal, focusing upon the goal, employing positive emotions, persisting in change strategies, maintaining change, using strengths, and the significance of attending to the better side of our humanity as the best strategy to transcend the human dilemmas that confront us all. Psychotherapy based on these research findings is a radical departure from the prevailing models of psychotherapeutic change.

Problem versus Goal Focus. The most fundamental flaw of the physical science metaphor of psychotherapy centers on the importance of the problem in psychotherapy. Historically, psychotherapy is based upon the premise that diagnosing or interpreting the meaning of the person's problem is central to treatment. Progress is based upon the clarity of the problem. The more exact the diagnosis the better the psychotherapy. Within a physical science metaphor, when problems are fixed, the machine operates again. This perspective makes sense because a problem cannot be fixed that is unknown or inaccessible in the physical science metaphor.

The psychological research on humans rather than machines reveals theory-shattering results! Focusing on the problem rather than the goal is detrimental to growth. The benefit of focusing on a positive goal in the approach- and avoidant-motivation literature unequivocally supports the superiority of focusing on a positive goal over a problem focus. *Approach motivation* means a focus on achieving a desired state. For example, a positive goal is: "I want to have a warm relationship with my son." *Avoidant motivation* focuses upon keeping the problem from occurring: "I do not want to fight with my son," or, "I don't want to think about my relationship with my son."

The approach-motivation research strongly supports the benefits of a positive goal orientation. Focusing on a positive goal, rather than avoiding a problem, increases a person's motivation and energy for actively achieving his or her goal (Goetz, Robinson, & Meier, 2008). Research participants under goal-focused conditions (in comparison to participants in problem-avoidant conditions) approach tasks with greater optimism as well as a greater commitment to learn new things, start something new, and try new and challenging activities.[2] The increased activity level and willingness to take risks directed toward a positive goal is essential in psychotherapy.

Focusing on a goal versus avoiding the problem is also accompanied by higher persistence toward an achievable goal (Dweck, 1999; Elliot, McGregor, & Gable, 1999). Pursuing positive goals facilitates novel and creative solutions instead of repetitive solutions that do not work. More solutions are generated and attempted with approach goals (Crowe & Higgins, 1997; Friedman & Forster, 2001).

Again, the translation to psychotherapy is straightforward. Achieving new accomplishments in life requires persistence *and* creativity. When something is not working, it is important to back away in order to attempt something else. The skill of knowing when to *hold* (i.e., persist) versus when to *fold* (i.e., find a new strategy; Lench & Levine, 2008) is enhanced when pursuing a positive goal rather than focusing on the problem. A signature quote of strategic therapy is that, "if at first you don't succeed, try

---

2. The reported research in positive psychology is primarily based upon laboratory research rather then therapy research.

something else" (Watzlawick, Weakland, & Fisch, 1974). In business circles, managers are urged to "work smarter, not just harder." Surprisingly, however, many people and therapists are unrelenting in using "more of the same" tactics. A problem-reduction focus seems to invite this rigidity. For example, if the family problem is defined as a rebellious daughter, no progress can be made until the daughter stops rebelling. If, however, the family goal is to have fun together, there are many ways for the daughter to participate in family attempts at reaching the goal of mutual enjoyment (remember equifinality).

People can, of course, manage their lives by avoiding problems. Surely, in some measure avoidant motivation is present in everyday life. There are consequences, however, that arise from a problem-avoidant focus. For example, even when successfully avoiding a problem, a person is left at best with feelings of relief and at worst with the negative emotions of anxiety and anger (Dweck, 1999; Lench & Levine, 2008). In contrast, a person who successfully achieves a positive goal feels good about the accomplishment (Carver, 2004; Elliot & Church, 2002; Higgins, Shah, & Friedman, 1997). This means that, if I manage to get through dinnertime without an argument with my son, I may feel relieved but also anxious about the next encounter and perhaps a bit angry that my dinnertimes are so tense. If, however, my son and I search websites together and have fun finding films and music to have on hand for a family reunion, I feel great about accomplishing the goal of increased closeness with him. Consider the energy, creativity, positive feeling, and willingness to re-engage in the web-search process that occurs in the latter example.

The positive feelings associated with goal attainment facilitate psycho-therapy success. Feeling good after achieving a goal leads to more energy for achieving additional goals. On the other hand, the feeling of relief upon successful avoidance of the problem does not provide energy to pursue more goals. I might engage in the intervention once but what keeps me using this skill?

Neither type of motivational style is always successful. Those who tend to use approach rather than avoidant strategies feel disappointed when they fail. Avoidant individuals experience more anger and anxiety when they are unsuccessful. This difference has some therapeutic implications. It is easier to maintain a relationship with someone who is disappointed than it is to maintain a relationship with an angry, anxious person. The disappointed person may be easier to approach and support. The angry person may not invite such connections. Because shared stories and conversations create family realities, approachability and support are vital ingredients to building new system strengths. The impressive research on the importance of having a positive goal to focus on clearly makes sense as we apply the results in psychotherapy. The attention focused on the positive goals of family therapy creates an environment favorable to good feelings and sociability.

Positive Affect. The experience of positive affect or emotion is a global indicator of how well we are doing—that is, our *subjective well-being*. The balance of positive to negative emotions we experience across a day is a marker of mental health functioning (Diener, Sandvik, & Pavot, 1991). Much of the extant literature in psychotherapy and psychology, however, has been focused on negative affect or negative emotions—for example, research on how to reduce fear and anxiety. Although it is clearly important to build interventions aimed at the direct reduction of negative emotions, very little attention has been paid to building positive affect as a psychotherapeutic strategy.[3] A growing research base supports the powerful effects of positive affect.

Most people understand that success leads to positive emotions. Few know, however, that the converse is true as well. Research indicates that positive emotions, such as happiness, cause successful outcomes (Fredrickson, 1998; Lyubomirsky, King, & Diener, 2005). Success leads to happiness and happiness leads to success. Therefore, positive family therapy includes positive emotions as a process as well as an outcome goal of psychotherapy. Many clients seen in family therapy come with marital, parenting, and work challenges. Finding that happiness leads to success in all these areas makes positive emotions a vital building block for a new approach to family therapy. Consider the following examples.

Happiness in marriages, measured by the ratio of positive to negative interactions, predicts long-lasting relationships (Gottman & Levenson, 1999). This means that couples who manage an interactional style that is characterized by caring, attentive, supportive statements to each other are unlikely to divorce and highly likely to report being happily married. The quality of the conversation between the two people creates a shared reality that defines their marriage as successful.

People who describe themselves as happy (i.e., high in positive affect and relatively low in negative affect) are socially more attractive to a wide variety of people (Kashdan & Roberts, 2004). They report being and are seen as more socially expert (Isen, 1999). Happy people are more sought after as friends and more likely to receive assistance from others when they are in need (Salovey, Rothman, Detweiler, & Steward, 2000). Positive affect

---

3. Joseph Wolpe's (1990) systematic desensitization is a notable exception where a positive affect, relaxation, is used to counter anxiety.

invites social interaction through smiles and laughter (Frijda & Mesquita, 1994; Keltner & Kring, 1998; Ruch, 1993). In marriage and friendship, happiness promotes successful relating. The research results outline an important circularity or recursive quality. Good marriages and friends make people happy, and happy people make good marriages and good friends.

Strong relationships or social support contributes to a person's subjective well-being, physical health, and emotional adjustment as well as creating more social acceptance and positive emotions (Argyle & Martin, 1991; Cohen, 1988; House, Landis, & Umberson, 1988; Myers, 1992). These findings reflect a long tradition of research. For example, Wilson reported in 1967, "Perhaps the most impressive single finding lies in the relation between happiness and successful involvement with people" (p. 304).

In 1962, Eric Fromm asserted that part of being a good mother was being a happy person because of the facilitative influence of happiness on healthy child development. More contemporary research supports the important role of positive affect in the parent-child attachment process. A smiling infant influences mothers to feel and act more positively (Fredrickson, 1998, 2001; Tomkins, 1962). Mothers who express more positive affect facilitate infant expression of positive affect (Haviland & Lelwica, 1987). Again, notice the circular influence of attachment and positive affect.

Positive affect influences success at work. Workers with high positive affect receive higher performance ratings from their supervisors and are viewed as more reliable and productive (Cropanzano & Wright, 1999; Staw, Sutton, & Pelled, 1994; Wright & Staw, 1999). Employees expressing more happiness receive higher ratings in goal emphasis, work facilitation, and teamwork (Wright & Staw, 1999).

In a comprehensive review of the literature on the influence of positive feelings such as happiness, Lyubomirsky, King, and Diener (2005) summarized the impressive results. Specifically, they found that happiness facilitated social relationships, healthy behavior, coping ability, and immune systems. Frequent feelings of happiness decreased stress, accidents, and suicide rates as well as enhanced our commitment to values or character development. Happy people are more altruistic, kind, and charitable. Positive emotions prevent drug abuse (Wills, Sandy, Shinar, & Yaeger, 1999) and problem drinking (Peterson, Seligman, Yurko, Martin, & Friedman, 1998).

The persuasive research on positive emotions demands center stage in psychotherapy. Positive emotions influence growth and sociability and are themselves worthy goals. Global research investigating levels of subjective well-being across nations supports the universal importance of happiness, but it also suggests that how different groups label or interpret happiness has some variation (Tov & Diener, 2007). For example, pride is a positive emotion in Australia and the United States, but more negatively viewed in China and Taiwan (Eid & Diener, 2001). Families are embedded in the macro-systems of culture and are themselves each different. Families create unique cultures requiring continual sensitivity.

Broaden and Build Model of Positive Emotions. Barbara Fredrickson (1998) developed a model of how positive emotions influence human development. A wide range of research has supported her model, the *Broaden and Build Theory.* Most importantly for us, her work directly supports the processes used in our approach to psychotherapy and is consistent with our theory of how change occurs.

The *Broaden and Build Theory* describes two primary functions that positive emotions serve. First, positive emotions *broaden* a person's thinking and behaviors. When experiencing positive emotions we are more likely to engage our world in a creative manner (Bryan & Bryan, 1991; Carnevale & Isen, 1986). Creative engagement broadens our behavioral repertoire, which gives us more ways to cope, and facilitates greater social involvement and knowledge. The second step, *build*, describes the expansion of social and intellectual skills that increases our array of abilities and social contacts supporting future growth. Finally, the outcome of broadening and building abilities results in our experiencing more positive feelings, which in turn leads to more broadening and building. This positive cycle of personal development with positive emotions escalates in a productive manner throughout our lives.

Fredrickson's model (1998) grew out of research in experimental personality psychology. Note the parallel of her findings with experimental research about approach motivation. Motivation to approach a goal increases personal resources of energy, motivation, and creativity. Positive affect increases personal resources in ways that attract additional resources. Applications to therapy are very promising. The consistent findings that positive affect facilitates growth as well as increasing cooperation and caring overlap with therapeutic goals for most families. For example, children involved in positive play experiences increase their physical, intellectual, and social resources. Therapy assignments that direct parents and children to play together begin a positive spiral of experiencing more positive emotions that in turn provide them with greater resources to accomplish a wide variety of family goals.

Research in positive psychology has underscored the importance of positive emotions on several important variables that influence child development including levels of prosocial behavior (Isen, Horn, & Rosenhan, 1973; Kenrick, Baumann, & Cialdini, 1979), cognition (Bryan &

Bryan, 1991), and memory (Bartlett, Burleson, & Santrock, 1982; Bugental, Lin, & Susskind, 1995; Duncan, Todd, Perlmutter, & Masters, 1985; Forgas, Burnham, & Trimboli, 1988). Happy children are more successful in all these arenas than are children with high levels of negative affect.

Hope. Positive psychology research has led to an increased focus on hope/optimism and other human virtues (e.g., McCullough & Snyder, 2000; Park, Peterson, & Seligman, 2006). Hope has received a great deal of recent empirical investigation. Results underscore its fundamental relationship to well-being (Snyder, 2002). Higher hope enhances mental health, recovery from major illnesses and injuries, academic performance, and athletic performance. Hope seems important in all aspects of life (Snyder, Lapointe, Crowson, & Early, 1998).

Successful family therapy must instill hope in family members. In therapy, hope is the belief that a person can accomplish her or his goals. A person who believes in her or his ability will initiate a plan and persevere through obstacles until reaching the goal. People with confidence in their abilities to succeed engage in more self-supportive statements such as, "I know I can do this" (Snyder et al., 1998).

Hope counters the pervasive demoralized feeling that is central to clients' pain (Frank & Frank, 2004). Snyder (1994, 2002) found that hope consists of believing that ways of accomplishing a goal can be discovered and the person has the ability to carry out the plan. Having multiple routes to attaining a goal increases a person's hope of accomplishing the goal because if one approach becomes blocked, another route is available— another parallel with the general system theory prediction of equifinality in open social systems.

Positive emotions consistently bolster immediate levels of hope and over time serve to establish higher long-term hope (Gallagher, 2008). Even watching a brief humorous film that makes us laugh out loud can increase our immediate feelings of hope (Fredrickson & Branigan, 2005). Research on interventions that bolster positive affect such as laughing out loud has direct translation into family therapy. When we engage with the family members with humor and positive visualizations of the family, positive affect is elicited. Even though the feelings of hope are transitory in the initial therapy session, the early experiences of progress contribute to the reciprocal nature of confidence and hope and positive emotions. After the family members begin to have confidence in their abilities to strategize together and accomplish their plans, hope replaces despair. The broaden-and-build process begins as positive feelings help clients initiate more activities that further build capacities and resources (Fredrickson, 1998; Gallagher, 2008).

For example, we could ask the family to tell us about a good time they had together. As they tell the story, we facilitate each person telling what was nice about it so as to increase each member's involvement in the experience. As the family members become more involved in the reporting of good times they have more positive feelings. The positive feelings increase hope. Hope means that they have more confidence in their ability to create this kind of family experience again. As therapists, we are excited and interested in their reports. Our interest and attention facilitate their talking more about the enjoyable family experience as well as promoting their positive feelings. We also ask about how the experience came about and if it can be recreated. We remind them about how each member contributed to the experience and how each can contribute to initiating a similar event in the near future. This kind of interaction reflects the model of social constructivism—a story is being constructed that creates a positive reality for the members to enjoy. Enjoying time together predicts they will be able to think more broadly about their experiences of being together and increases the chances they can build future positive interactions. Very specifically, assigning this conversation as a task in family therapy does the following:

1. It helps the family remember or discover multiple ways to reach their goal because each member of the system contributes.
2. It gives the therapist multiple opportunities to remind the family of how actions are linked to goals and why goals are important.
3. It gives the therapist opportunities to point out how the family has been able to accomplish part or all of similar goals/behaviors in the past.

How Change Occurs: The Basics

All psychological theories of change are reductionistic because to be helpful they must oversimplify the complexity of life. The ecological, historical, developmental, biological, and psychological complexities of people, especially people in relation to other people as in a family, present an overwhelming number of possible change targets, strategies, and levels to a therapist. Therefore, each psychological theory takes a part of the human picture to focus upon with the understanding that the particular perspective is likely to be helpful in supporting change. However, the means to the end is important as well. We appreciate that theoretical support for Positive Family Therapy means using positive emotions, sociability, and virtues to achieve an end.

The change theory consistent with systems thinking and the positive psychology broaden-and-build model has been called *escalation, deviation-amplifying,* or *positive feedback theory* (Maruyama, 1963). *Escalation theory* describes the process of how a small change can lead to a much larger change in the system. Many major systems theorists have made use of escalation theory as a way to understand change (i.e., Watzlawick et al., 1974; de Shazer, 1982; Bateson, 1972; Sluzki & Beavin, 1965; Maruyama, 1963; Wender, 1968; Boscolo, Cecchin, Hoffman, & Penn, 1987).

Escalation sequences assume that wittingly or unwittingly people respond to each other in a manner that is met with a response of greater emotional intensity. The response is based upon each respondent's understanding of the situation—his/her beliefs or attributions or constructions. Beliefs, attributions, past history, and constructions are encapsulated into the term *meaning system*. Each person responds from his or her own meaning system as the escalation occurs. Because people act within their own personal meaning system, each feels reasonable or justified in their actions because it makes sense to them. It is quite common for people to misunderstand each other's motives.

We do not propose that escalation theory describes how a problem develops (although it could). Escalation theory's strengths lie in its ability to describe the process of change in a manner that is inclusive and mutually beneficial. The theory allows for different constructions of the solution toward a mutual goal. Escalation theory describes how a system intensifies its processes over time. Escalation can lead to by-products that are experienced as enjoyable or terrible. An escalating interaction results in heightened intensity of feelings, behaviors, and/or beliefs based upon deeply entrenched attribution (meanings) held by the participants.

For a clearer understanding of escalation at work, imagine a couple sitting together on the couch. Person A smiles warmly at person B. B returns the smile and pats A's hand. A kisses B's hand. B leans over to kiss A on the cheek. And on goes the interactions that increase in positive intensity from the perspective of both A and B. The process, which started with a smile, could end with passionate intercourse. The escalation process was maintained by a mutual construction of the process as communicating caring and desire to feel close to one another. Both persons understood each communication as information consistent with a welcomed and increasingly intense message of love.

A family system will have many complex issues and interactions occurring simultaneously. The assessment and change process is complex. The pattern of escalation is not exactly predictable in a family—we must deal with probabilities.

Research Support of Escalation Theory.   The research on the accuracy of how escalation describes change is not as convincing as we would like. The support for escalation theory is based upon the reported effectiveness of therapeutic approaches based upon escalation theory, research on reciprocity of communication, and conceptual helpfulness of escalation theory. Techniques derived from escalation theory have case and best practice clinical support (e.g., de Shazer, 1982; Fisch, Weakland, & Segal, 1982).

Research on reciprocity of action between people grew from Thibaut and Kelley's (1959) social exchange theory of social relationships. *Social exchange theory* represents relationships in economic terms. The satisfaction or worth of the relationship is a function of the benefits received and the cost incurred. Patterson (1982) developed a similar description through his behavioral orientation. Of special importance to family therapists are Patterson's evidence-based descriptions of problematic escalation patterns called *reciprocal coercion*.

Studies on marital interactions revealed interactional sequences with characteristics predicted by escalation theory. A positive or negative behavior is likely to be followed by a behavior of the like kind from a spouse (Billings, 1979; Gottman, 1979; Gottman, Markman, & Notarius, 1977; Margolin & Wampold, 1981; Raush, Barry, Hertel, & Swain, 1974; Hahlweg, Revenstorf, & Schindler, 1984; Schaap, 1984). Also, these studies indicated that negative interactional sequences are more likely to occur with distressed couples than with nondistressed couples. Revenstorf and colleagues' (1984) study found that nondistressed couples were more likely to reciprocate positive behavior.

Jacobson and colleagues' (1982) and Gottman (1976) found distressed couples more likely to react immediately with negative communications toward each other. Partners were more likely to respond negatively to each other to begin escalation cycles when they were distressed.

Hahlweg and colleagues (1984) examined the type and number of escalation sequences of couples in therapy. They found that negative escalation was decreased after therapy. Positive escalation (he called this *attractive escalation*) occurred more often and with more sequences in nondistressed couples than with distressed couples. After therapy, positive escalation was more frequent and had a greater number of sequences. The posttherapy improvement surpassed even the nondistressed comparison group.

The Shortcomings of the Escalation Model.   Escalation as a metaphor of the change process in people's interrelationships has dangers. Because escalation originates from the physical sciences, there may be a tendency to mechanize our application with people. For example, people will not escalate every time, nor will they do so in identical ways over time. No exponential curve can be plotted that describes the typical escalation sequence, but some patterns do emerge. Most adult children can identify how visiting their aging parents elicits old patterns of behavior—some pleasant and some not. These patterns have been called *dances* (Lerner, 1985, 1989) and can revolve around anger or intimacy, dependency or independence, criticism or valuing. While predictable, they are not inevitable and are open to adjustment.

Further, it is important to know that escalation does not reduce responsibility for the abusive or dangerous behavior of a particular family member. Aggression is not "caused" by lower intensity prompts from others. The escalation metaphor helps us look for a systemic understanding but it does not relieve aggressive members of accountability for their actions. If an abusive situation is presented, we expect to find an interaction that prompts the aggression (e.g., often alcohol intake by the abuser or some small "transgression" from a child or spouse). We expect this interaction to be described differently by each member of the system. These descriptions of interrelated events allow for an uncovering of many sources of influence that prevent the family from reaching satisfactory levels of security. An exploration can uncover a host of issues and influences that may be useful in moving a family toward safety. In these situations, family members may be engaged in a dangerous, escalating "blame game."

Escalation theory can help along the road to systemic thinking but it is not the end point. Many ways of understanding systemic thinking facilitate our abilities to help our clients. Also, we find that concentrating on the escalation of positive emotions and sociable goals avoids inadvertent misuses of the theory.

Escalation Theory and First- and Second-Order Change. Consider a child making poor grades. Initially, the parents scold the child for making the low grades. The child makes poorer grades. The parents demand that the child study in the evenings with no television. The child's grades worsen. The parents do not let the child play with friends after school. The child quits completing any schoolwork. The grades plummet further and the parents find new punishments. The parents' best attempts to focus the child's attention on academic success, while somewhat reasonable, are unsuccessful. Their very common escalating change dilemma introduces us to the concepts of first- and second-order change.

Notice that a compelling aspect of the escalation sequence described between the parents and their homework-avoidant child is that each intensified move by the parents is more-of-the-same and is met with an intensified more-of-the-same response from the child. Like many humans, these parents have followed a well-known dictum that, if the desired reaction is not gained by the first change attempt, then "try, try, again." Watzlawick, Weakland, and Fisch (1974) describe this as a first-order change attempt. That is, when a desired outcome is not accomplished our tendency is to try harder within the same problem-solving model.

When the parents from the previous example report on their efforts, they are likely to say that they have tried "everything." But an attentive therapist will realize that all the attempts are actually derivatives of one or two themes. Perhaps the parents believe their parental job is to introduce children to the consequences of the real world—bad things happen to people who fail to live up to their responsibilities. The punishment sequence is designed to be sure the child will eventually achieve success as a responsible adult. Although the parents imagine they have used many strategies, they have used just one strategy at increasing levels of intensity. "Negative consequences will change behavior" was the only strategy. They have used a first-order change logic.

Second-order change implies a fundamental or significant break with past and current practices. Second-order change requires new knowledge and skills for successful implementation (Fraser & Solovey, 2006). Continuing the example of the child with poor grades, imagine a change strategy that disrupts the parents' (and the child's) view of responsibility and the demands of good parenting. In our first example, the parents became the present transmitters of the cold cruel world their child is doomed to face.

What if their understanding of poor grades and homework completion was not based on irresponsibility, but on the child's inadequate skills or their child's motivation to be noticed for other skills? What other strategies might they attempt? Perhaps their first intervention would be to set up an after-dinner parent and child homework club during which both child and parents read, did paperwork, and discussed any challenges they faced. If unsuccessful, another nonincremental strategy would be to focus on the child's strengths and accomplishments. Although the homework club might continue, the parents would carve out time to pay attention to the child's athletic, artistic, or social accomplishments. A third attempt might be to include other young people in the homework club—increasing social support for attention to work.

Instead of relying on escalating levels of discomfort to teach responsibility, the parents could use increasing levels of social support and attention to illustrate useful strategies in surmounting difficult life challenges—

ask for help, compensate with strengths, seek other avenues to increase motivation. This approach has the added advantage of providing the child with a view of his or her future that is based on a build-and-broaden strategy. When faced with a challenge, seek strategies that increase positive affect.

The use of first-order change—that is, the one-solution set that escalates with continually worsening outcomes—was seen as the hallmark of human difficulty by Fisch, Weakland, and Segal (1982). Fisch and colleagues developed a change procedure that defined the client's solution as the problem. Their goal was to get the client to stop the current solution attempts because the attempts were escalating the situation. *Pathology* occurred when clients made two mistakes: selecting an unhelpful solution activity and then sticking with it (Fisch et al., 1982). We have noticed that most successful second-order change interventions would fit with the predictions from the positive psychology literature. For example, a favorite intervention of Fisch and colleagues is to have the parents buy the child a dog because the presence of a pet very often leads to positive affect.

SUMMARY

Chapter One introduced historical and current research and theory in systems theory and positive psychology. The selected information supports the model of Positive Family Therapy that follows in the next chapters. Now that the foundation formed by theory and constructs has been laid, the techniques and applications follow. We sense your growing positive emotions such as curiosity, hope, and laughter. You should know that every subsequent chapter creates more positive feeling. Really!

CHAPTER 2

Techniques in Positive
Family Therapy

GOAL OF CHAPTER 2

There are many family therapy strategies that have been tried by clinicians and some that have been tested in rigorous research. This chapter presents the therapeutic techniques that are consistent with a positive family systems approach and specifies which have evidence or best practice support. These are presented with exemplars in a rough sequence of when they might be most useful in therapy. The techniques are based upon our own research, experimental personality and social psychology research in positive psychology, and traditional family therapy techniques that are consistent with the goals of Positive Family Therapy.

Key concepts in Chapter 2: both/and logic versus either/or logic, circular questioning, Columbo technique, complimenting, congruence, enactment, empathy, finding exceptions, interrupting, joining, miracle question, neutrality, paraphrasing, parent as model, punctuation, rapport building, reflection, reframing, scaling questions, therapeutic alliance, unconditional positive regard.

OVERVIEW

The techniques of Positive Family Therapy are designed to involve each family member in the construction of a new family reality so that each person recognizes a responsibility for the success of every other family member and her/himself. The family unit, however defined (two parents or one, straight or gay members, childless or rich with children from numerous sources), typically offers the most significant life influence for each member. The family forms a culture—a web of shared stories—that shapes each individual. This web of shared meaning makes the family ideal for supporting growth.

The general outline of therapy is that each person is invited to contribute and each person is reminded repeatedly that he or she has the influence to make a difference in the family's development. The techniques to be presented are meant to clarify the family's values and goals, as well as build upon their strengths. Family members are asked to imagine how they would like the family to function. Each person is helped to present a perspective and is reassured that therapists expect each perspective to be unique—that is, the family is a social construction. The overarching goals of families are, however, inevitably similar. Families exist to offer nurturing environments to each member, to communicate and preserve values and virtues particular to a family, and to help each family member reach optimal levels of personal attainment.

As the family moves toward each member's goals, the problems prompting therapy are alleviated. The focus is on what the individuals want to have happen instead of what they want stopped. Change is self-sustaining because the family goal is beyond problem elimination. The family's commitment to change does not stop when the problem subsides. The change is embraced as continuously building toward new goals using the acquired skills and the associated positive feelings. When growth is the goal, blame becomes much less relevant. Successful Positive Family Therapy ends with everyone in the family feeling happier.

INITIAL RAPPORT BUILDING AND STRENGTH FINDING

Similar to all types of psychotherapy, the initial contact between the therapist and the family requires gaining trust, influence, and information about each individual. The standard therapeutic techniques that build rapport include asking questions, paraphrasing, and summarizing. There are some differences between standard approaches and Positive Family Therapy initial approaches, however. In Positive Family Therapy, the therapist is interested in each member's strengths and not in-depth analysis of a presenting problem. The interest is communicated by what clients content the therapist chooses to paraphrase, summarize, and pursue with questions. The strengths of the individuals receive more focus than do complaints or problems.

Many family members are surprised by focusing on the positive and try to influence the therapist to hear their stories of complaints—hoping no doubt to get the therapist on their "side" in the family dilemma. In most models of therapy (based as they are on a physical science metaphor), the therapist focuses upon the family's shortcomings and problems in order to be helpful. There is, however, a price to this approach. The minimum cost is the time wasted examining the details of the problems. The more significant problem is the potential harm that arises from highlighting family inadequacies—for example, parenting problems or negative child behaviors. In both cases, family members experience negative affect and often a desire to avoid a conversation about failures. Also, the way to prove a negative story is correct is by provoking the negative behavior to a greater extent. Both the negative affect and the avoidance predict less energy, hopefulness, and creativity toward a better functioning family.

In contrast, a focus upon the family strengths has none of these problematic features. The therapist listens with interest as the family tells of their concerns but enthusiastically responds to the family's descriptions of good times, abilities, and goals. The therapist's questions and reactions communicate clearly his or her beliefs about the family. It is axiomatic that people like people who like them. The Positive Family Therapy practitioner communicates a strong liking for the family as a high-functioning and successful entity.

Positive Family Therapists often begin the initial therapy session by explaining the process of therapy to reduce family members' anxiety and increase their cooperation. The first stage of therapy is getting to know something about each family member. Each member is asked what could make the family even better. The therapist reminds each member that he or she is seeking a personal assessment. There may be many different thoughts, although it is also common that family members need help to stay positive and not return to problem elimination as the goal of therapy.

Letting the members know that the focus will be on their goals instead of their problems is a key message. We often say something like, "The problems let us know that some things in your family may not be going well, but the problems do not tell us what you want, only what you do not want." Family therapy consists of figuring out what they want and how to accomplish what they want in ways that promote family happiness.[1] Therefore, the discussions primarily will be about what they want now and in the future. The past will not be the focus of therapy except to find out what they do well so that strengths can be amplified.

---

1. The promotion of family happiness needs to be explored at some point with the family to see if this positive emotion is consistent with the family culture.

Rapport Building / Joining / Interrupting

The first step in rapport building is briefly getting to know each person. Often we begin with the youngest but we may skip a person who seems difficult to engage (e.g., the adolescent who is identified as the family problem). "What is your name? How old are you? What grade are you in school? What is your favorite subject? What do you do for fun?" We express interest in and are complimentary toward each person. From the beginning we are more excited about and attentive to strengths that are revealed. Strengths are anything that is enjoyable, valued, or done well. Usually we ask about the parents last. We ask about age and laugh because of the awkwardness. We ask about work and blended family issues. Who is the biological parent? Who are the caretaking parents?

Early interactions with the family members allow them to build impressions of the therapist and to make some predictions about what to expect in therapy. The initial conversations are the basis for *joining* with the family. This process of rapport building, joining, or building an alliance between the therapist and the family is critical. It is critical because the family must come to view the therapist as competent and trustworthy if therapy is to succeed.

Carl Rogers's (1957) conditions of congruence, unconditional positive regard, and empathy provide the gold standard in creating open, trusting, therapeutic relationships or alliances. *Congruence* refers to presenting our real selves as we communicate with the family members. *Unconditional positive regard* involves "a warm acceptance of each aspect of the client's experience as being a part of the client . . . no conditions of acceptance, no feeling of 'I like you only if you are thus and so'" (Rogers, 1957, p. 97). *Empathy* occurs when the therapist can "sense the client's anger, fear or confusion as if it were your own, yet without your own anger, fear or confusions getting bound up in it" (Rogers, 1957, p. 99). While it is impossible to be perfect at these lofty conditions with all family members all the time, each necessary and sufficient attribute gives therapists an interpersonal goal that facilitates clients coming to see therapists as competent and trustworthy. Therapists should not underestimate the power of a therapeutic communication style based on congruence, unconditional positive regard, and empathy. Most people have never been in a therapeutic conversation and many are amazed at the power of the experience. Applications of these skills in positive family therapy have some special conditions.

Empathy provides an invaluable connection between people through the process of feeling understood or known by the other person. Further, once we are known and we feel safe with the person who knows us, we become more open, more flexible, more trusting in the relationship.

Positive Family Therapy uses empathy with a slightly different perspective than most other therapies. In this approach, empathic responses are not merely mirrors of what has been said. Multiple strands of meaning within a client statement can be pursued. Therapists choose which strands of a client's statement are most important. In family therapy the goal is to deepen the positive relationships between family members. The therapist's empathic response must open up communication pathways for other family members to use as they attempt to create more productive conversations. Shared empathy facilitates the family's functioning. To help a family reach shared empathy, the therapist responds to family members by picking up on both a vulnerable feeling and the goal orientation embedded within a client's statement. By responding to both, family members are invited to talk among themselves about a goal, not just a problem statement. For example, consider the following excerpt from a positive family session:

FATHER: I come home every day to a house in chaos. The children are running around and climbing on the furniture. Elisa is talking on the phone. I am exhausted from work and then facing this when I get home. I blow up.

THERAPIST: I am sorry that this is so frustrating Rafael, so difficult. I can hear by your tone that you do not want to 'blow up.' You would like to share another part of yourself when you get home. You would like for your relationship with your children and wife to be different as you return from work. What would you imagine it being like? How would you like to talk with your children and wife?

The therapist's statement is designed to communicate a deep understanding of Rafael. Touching on his frustration and then moving to his dreams of how it could be at home moves the conversation toward goals. As Rafael begins to state his goals for being close, his family members begin to experience him differently. Finding mutual goals becomes possible. As Rafael responds, however, he is likely to insert blaming statements about how his wife and children stop him from reaching his goals for a close family life.

FATHER: Well sure I want something different—everyone does. But it's just impossible with the mess and the noise I face every afternoon.

When the therapist hears or anticipates that problem focus or blaming is about to begin, the therapist should interrupt—despite the discomfort this causes for us because as therapists we think of ourselves as "good listeners." Family progress toward embracing positive goals rather than blame depends on keeping a new kind of conversation alive among the family members. An important therapeutic goal is to reduce conversations that use hurt as a change strategy. Interrupting counterproductive processes is a vital technique. Such interruptions may be rare in individual or problem-focused therapies, but they are very common in Positive Family Therapy.

THERAPIST: Help me understand what you want a little better. Now you want to be able to talk with your children? Right? How do you want to be feeling when you are talking with them?

A therapist can pair the interruption with a compliment.

THERAPIST: Wait a minute! Wait a minute! Just a second. Slow down. You have said some very important things that I need to think about for a minute. This is going too fast for me to get it all. Let's stop and let me think.

Interrupting early in the very first session lets everyone know that the therapist's job is to interrupt. It is not rude! Some therapists warn the family at the outset of therapy that they will need to interrupt often as a tool to gain an accurate understanding of the family and be as helpful as possible. This prediction of the process alerts the family to expect that therapy will provide some new ways of relating.

Applying Rogers's (1957) insights around unconditional positive regard and congruence in family therapy requires that therapists be very nimble in connecting with each member of the family during the first session. One family member may attempt to dominate the conversation and to speak for the others. In fact, the whole family may expect one person to do all the talking for them. The therapist must be sure, however, that each person has had a chance to speak and the opportunity to begin the trust-building process with the therapist. Success in making this happen depends on additional techniques.

NEUTRALITY

The construct of neutrality describes the basic stance or way of viewing therapeutic relations with a family (Boscolo et al., 1987). *Neutrality* means the therapist is interested in each person and each person's perspective and anticipates developing new perspectives from the synergy of shared stories among the members. When neutral, the therapist sequentially "sides with" each person in the system. Neutrality helps the therapist avoid becoming attached to a single viewpoint of how the system functions (Cecchin, 1987). Neutrality does not mean an aloofness or absence of relationship with the individuals.[2] Neutrality is the balancing of the therapist's involvement among the members of the system. As we ask about the varying viewpoints of the members of a system we begin to discover a complex network of meaning. A neutral therapist balances both the gathering of and communicating about the family's story. The goal of neutrality is for the members of the family to feel that the therapist has not taken sides with any one person but has sided with—that is, understood with acceptance—all members. The therapist's curiosity and acceptance of multiple explanations about the family sets a new framework for a family conversation because in most families only one or two family views get airtime (Boscolo et al., 1987; Cecchin, 1987). The therapist can facilitate change in the family's typical first-order conversations by getting new information into the family's story.

The timing of speaking with each person is important. The movement should be timed to keep everyone interested and involved. Even while focusing upon one person, other family members can be included through circular questions. Neutrality is expressed by the inclusion of and attention to each individual. The very common therapeutic strategies of making eye contact, leaning forward toward the speaker, asking follow-up questions, and connecting some aspect of the speaker's comments to previous information are all ways to communicate inclusion. Further, in Positive Family Therapy, the therapist looks for a strength to reflect or insert into each initial interaction. For example, even if the first interaction with a reluctant teen has been strained the therapist might say the following before moving on quickly to the next family member:

THERAPIST: Thanks for telling me about school and your hobbies. Having someone your age in our conversation is vital, you know. Most adults sort of forget what those years are like. We need an expert like you.

When family members are ill at ease with therapy, we visit with them about their strengths for an extended time. In contrast, if a family is upset and communicates a desire for quick progress, we spend less time on initial rapport building, but we always attempt collecting something positive about each family member within the first 30 minutes of a session. This information is critical.

---

2. Neutrality as defined by Boscolo et al. (1987) is very different than the psychodynamic construct.

Punctuating the Positive or Focusing on Strengths

There are several strategies therapists use to keep the family's focus on their strengths and facilitate positive affect. This focus on family strength is critical to keep the family's energy high, motivation strong, and hopes elevated. The basic way the therapist *punctuates*, or pulls the family's attention toward its own strengths, is focusing his or her energetic attention to particular aspects of the family's story. Special energy is needed because there are some contextual threats to the family's ability to feel strong in therapy.

For example, many therapists are from more privileged ethnic/racial backgrounds, sexual orientations, religious groups, gender, language groups, or socioeconomic status than are their clients. Without attention to these discrepancies, societal patterns of dominance and submission can inadvertently be recreated in the therapy room. Clients from less privileged backgrounds can feel degraded by a therapy that asks them to delve deeply into their problems. The problem-identification process can feel like a retraumatization of past discrimination experiences. A therapeutic process that focuses on strengths avoids the pitfalls of clients' perceiving our zeal to understand their problems as evidence that we are attempting to justify our privileged status. Families in distress may need help, however, in identifying strengths.

Past successes mark strength. Any reports of good times or good feelings in the past deserve therapist attention. Clients may not know their strengths or see the fact that past occurrences of good times are predictors of the future, but the therapist can insert that notion. For example:

MOTHER: I don't know what has happened. When Juan went to school, at first the teachers all loved him because he was so smart. Now all I hear are complaints.

THERAPIST: So when Juan started school, he was the smartest boy in his class. You must have been very proud of him. I wonder if he remembers being proud of himself. Do you recall being the star, Juan?

Complimenting family members highlights strengths as well. As de Jong and Berg (1998) assert,

Complimenting should not be motivated by a desire to be kind to clients. Instead, it should be reality-based, in the sense that it is derived from what the client communicates to you through words or client process. (1998, p. 31)

Clients need accurate information about their strengths so that they can build upon them. Compliments should be used strategically, however, because compliments are evaluative statements. A few compliments reveal that we are interested in family strengths. Too many compliments communicate a large hierarchical difference between the therapist and family members. In addition, specific comments are much more powerful than general complimentary statements. "You told me you were 6, but you just answered that question with words like you were an 8 year old. I'm impressed." This statement is a much better use of a positive evaluation than the vague, "Good job!"

When clients are exhibiting behaviors or describing past behaviors that we believe can contribute to accomplishing their goals, then we can respond with a positive reaction and underscore a link between behavior and goal with a question.

JUAN: I used to care more about school, but now I'm just planning to make some money so I can buy things.

THERAPIST: That is great that you are a planner. I wonder how you can use that ability of being a good planner to help you reach the family goal of making better grades?

At times, family strengths are punctuated by the therapist acting dumb. Sometimes called the *Columbo technique,* the therapist engages in a series of questions asking for clarification of what seems to be an obvious point. In this way, current family strengths and the links between the strengths and desired goals can be underscored.

THERAPIST: Now how will planning ahead help with your getting better grades?

JUAN: I am not sure, but I guess it helps with getting assignments done.

THERAPIST: I wonder if other members of your family are good planners. Did you inherit that from somebody? Do you see how anyone else in the family is as good a planner as you are?

JUAN: My mother is the family plan person. She always has a list so that when we shop we never forget anything. She also has a big calendar so that she knows where we have to be.

THERAPIST: So good planning and record keeping is a family skill. I wonder if your Mom's lists and calendar could be used to help you in school?

Repetitive questions that link the change idea (better planning) to the goal (better grades) help the clarity of the plan. Stating the idea and the goal clearly provides a review of the goal and facilitates hope by emphasizing the inevitability of progress. When one member of the family has an insight about a change that could lead toward reaching family goals, the therapist is responsible for making certain everyone in the family understands so that the change can be as wide reaching as possible.

JUAN: I don't know for sure, but I do know that I lose points on my assignments when I forget them or they are late. If I had lists and a calendar like my Mom, I guess I'd do better.

THERAPIST: Sounds like you are good at planning—maybe you did inherit it from your Mom.

Therapists model excitement to encourage family members to do the same. Asking other family members directly or indirectly to recognize each other's insights can be important.

THERAPIST: Wow that was a great idea, Juan! Mom, thanks for being the source of all this planning skill. By the way, how does your family show enthusiasm for a wonderful idea like Juan just had? Hugs, high fives?

When a family member reports a good week (or even a good day!), we respond with intensity and curiosity.

THERAPIST: Wonderful, Chelsea! What happened for you to say that it was a nice week?

Any report of progress should be examined in detail so that everyone knows progress occurred. Careful analysis of good examples facilitates knowing how to recreate and expand upon the success.

THERAPIST: Now how did you do that? How did that happen? Did you know you could do that? Is that something you can continue to do?

Attention to progress made by family members clearly communicates the therapeutic belief that change is possible based on strengths that exist within the family. Family members begin to attend to their successes and understand how to support each other's efforts toward progress. Significant research in positive psychology points to the power of selective attention on the blessings of life in contrast to the negative outcomes associated with ruminating on the failures (e.g., Gable, Reis, Impett, & Asher, 2004; Koole, Smeets, van Knippenberg, & Dijksterhuis, 1999). We are what we think.

Positive emotions are significant strengths. The Broaden and Build Theory (Fredrickson, 1998) explains the ways positive emotions facilitate creative thinking and perseverance in reaching goals. Therefore, when the therapist hears a family member express positive emotions, these must be reflected and accentuated. Expressions of caring between family members are treasures.

THERAPIST: You do? You do love your mother? Does your mother know you love her? Haley, did you know Michael loves you? Wow. That is great!

On the other hand, negative feelings are not treasures. They are typically regarded as psychological hot potatoes that are moved over quickly. Old family problems and escalating processes lurk around most negative feelings. Families in therapy do not need more practice talking about failure and disappointment.

THE FAMILY'S PROBLEMATIC ISSUES

Families do enter therapy, however, with a strong motivation to fix something. Their family problem functions as a signal that there is a need for change. Many families enter therapy using a familiar medical practice perspective. Do you recall bringing your child to a pediatrician? The pressure to be able to recount exact symptoms, timing, attempted solutions, and child responses was very strong. Good parents can do that. Families anticipate the same in family therapy. They come ready with extensive records of failures and chronic problems. Their very reasonable and predictable hope is that careful problem description will lead to a particular prescription for a family cure.

What most families do not know upon beginning therapy is that problem descriptions do not signal family goals or exact pathways to change. Thus, they are surprised and, at times, a bit resistant when the therapist moves them rather quickly toward formulating a goal for therapy. Some of the astonishment can be reduced by using the initial telephone contact as preparation for focusing on a goal. While receiving the basic telephone information about the family and the issues to be addressed, therapists or their assistants can describe Positive Family Therapy.

THERAPIST: My approach to family therapy is to focus upon what you want as a family and to use your family's strengths to accomplish those goals. I know that you want the problem to go away, but what we have discovered is that it is vital to first discover how you want your family to be. I know you want to move away from the problem, but all of us will need to know what direction you want to move in. My job will be to help you use your strengths to accomplish those goals.

The therapist can ask the caller to be the initial expert on Positive Family Therapy. This can be accomplished by suggesting that he or she share this message with the family. Notice how this statement inserts a strong belief in the client's strengths even before therapy begins.

Therapist: I really appreciate this opportunity to talk with you about your family and know that your call indicates how much you care about the family's future. Will you do me the favor of talking to all the family members about our conversation? I think you will be the best person to explain to them what they should expect when we start.

No matter how well we prepare clients, however, some or all of them want to talk about problems. Listening to the problematic issues in the family is important for building a therapeutic alliance, but it is a bit tricky. The therapist wants to know what the problems are but must avoid blaming and spending unnecessary time on negative interaction patterns. Solution Focused therapists champion a technique that avoids long blame narratives (e.g., de Shazer et al., 2007). The therapist learns about the family by asking each person what they hope will happen in therapy. This approach is an effective strategy to minimize blaming and move toward goal setting.

Therapist: What do you hope will happen in therapy?

The therapist hopes the question and his or her response to the answers introduces a number of vital concepts to the therapy conversation:

1. There are different constructions and social constructions of problems and solutions.
2. Multiple perspectives or solutions are valuable as a way to enrich the family's story as a well-functioning family.
3. Careful listening with follow-up questions uncovers new material while communicating respect and caring.
4. There are alternatives to the blaming or hopeless processes that caused the family to seek help.

Some family members may try to move the focus back to long-winded problem descriptions. It is important not to spend too much time on any one person. A possible redirection is to say:

THERAPIST: I can tell that there is a lot of history to this issue. Tonight I want to just hear a little bit about these issues and what you want to accomplish. This will help us know where to start, perhaps.

Therapists must establish the norm that everyone gets the opportunity to speak. This sets the stage for neutrality. Not every person has to speak the same amount. For example, in most families the parents feel primarily responsible for providing the information in the first session and so they should be given the first opportunity to answer this question. In fact, most family cultures support parental leadership in setting the direction for the family and so should be honored by the therapist.

Therefore, although therapists listen respectfully to the problems described by family members, they show just enough interest to be polite and then move the person to describe his or her hopes for the therapy experience. The therapist also can ask all family members to imagine their family 6 months in the future or to describe their family without the identified family problem.

Some family cultures are such that parents are not used to listening to the children (or to one particularly troubling child). If this is the case, during the children's presentations of their perspectives, the parents should be complimented about the children's contributions, if possible. The needed balance the therapist must accomplish early in the course of therapy is to respect enough of the family's expectations so as to establish the therapeutic alliance while helping them move away from unhelpful, ingrained patterns of interaction that have kept them locked in a problem-focused stalemate.

THERAPIST: These ideas about how the family might function in the future really show what a strong family you have been building. Everyone seems to have some good insights about happy family life. Congratulations, parents, on providing this vision for the kids!

PARAPHRASING AND SUMMARIZING

Paraphrasing and summarizing are important techniques in therapy. *Paraphrasing* the client's statement means restating or repeating the most important content or meaning of the client's statement. Paraphrasing occurs after the client has stated one to three sentences. The therapist's restatement should be shorter than the client's statement. *Summarizing* is similar to paraphrasing but a summary restates more client statements and includes some of the therapist's paraphrases.

The techniques of paraphrasing and summarizing serve at least four major purposes in a session. First, these techniques can reassure the client that she or he is being understood and listened to carefully. After a restatement, we should pay careful attention to the client's reaction so that we know the client felt understood. Often a paraphrase or summary is ended with the question, "Am I right?" If the client disputes the paraphrase, this gives us a chance to seek more information.

Second, the techniques communicate what was important to the therapist about the client's communication. Not all of the information a client states is restated or summarized. The selection signals to the client what the therapist is thinking. The restatement of the family member's words can often reflect a slight change toward a more diplomatic statement, a slight reframing of the issue (reframing is described later in this chapter), and a more direct focus on the goal, solution, or strength communicated in the statement. This focus in the restatement communicates to the family members what the therapist sees as most important for progress.

Third, the techniques model effective listening. The family learns from the way the therapist interacts with them. The way the therapist communicates is an implicit message to the family that says, "This is the way successful adults act!"

Fourth, they are techniques that keep the therapy process flowing under the influence of the therapist. Families must be safe with the therapist and this means that the therapist takes responsibility for the conduct of the session. Paraphrasing and summarizing coupled with a willingness to interrupt and keep a focus on strengths gives the therapist significant control of a therapy session.

This fourth point may be somewhat surprising. The therapist's influence in the therapy session has been an important source discussion in the literature (Anderson, 1997; Hoffman, 1995; McNamee & Gergen, 1992; Sutherland, 2007). In Positive Family Therapy, clients' autonomy is respected. Each member of the family is seen as uniquely constructing both a self and a self in relation to others. The therapist must, however, provide a therapeutic structure for these multiple selves and selves in relation to each other to develop new meanings that write a new family story consistent with the family's goal.

This therapeutic structure is built from theory, techniques, and the personal attributes of the therapist. Making the therapy process overt by explaining how and why we exert influence processes allows clients to make informed evaluations about our therapy. When our clients understand, approve, and accept influence they will stay in therapy based on an informed choice.

CIRCULAR QUESTIONS

Circular questioning is the interviewing technique used to involve the entire family in considering an issue (Penn, 1982, 1985; Tomm, 1987a, 1987b, 1988; Boscolo et al., 1987). Circular questions are so named because they are designed to take information the therapist gained from the family and return it to the family again in order to inform the family and to gain more information for the therapist to again send into the family. Involving the entire family builds on the systemic strength of the whole being more than the sum of its parts (von Bertalanffy, 1976). The enriched conversation begins to create new perspectives, new solutions.

Like all questions, circular questions can function as assessment techniques. Circular questions, are however, also interventions (Penn, 1982, 1985; Tomm, 1987a, 1987b, 1988; Boscolo et al., 1987; Scheel, 1994). Reintroducing ideas back into the family prompts the family to add to the perspective. Circular questions also support neutrality by including all the perspectives in the family. No perspective should attain an ability to silence the others. Perspectives that are banished from the family banish the person as well. Excluding a member should be a conscious, carefully considered step for a family.

A circular question transforms an individual's statement into a more systemic influence by the circular question's content and the inclusion of other family members. The therapist moves from an intrapersonal stance to an interpersonal or interactional stance. The new perspective should respect the integrity of the original information stated by the individual family members, but the therapist's restatement provides new opportunities for solutions or goals. Bateson (1972, 1974) described this type of change as the difference between information and data. *Data* are defined as knowledge that everyone already knows. *Information* is useful in change because it adds something new.

The circular questioning techniques are specifically designed to uncover and inform the family members about differences. Differences are more likely to contain information for family growth and the family learns not to fear differences. In Positive Family Therapy, circular questions inquire about differences within the family in a curious, upbeat manner that uncovers strengths or goals.

A circular question risks violating neutrality. The introduction of a perspective may be viewed as taking sides in the family (Scheel & Conoley, 1998). A theme of the circular question may fit with the perspective suggested by some members of the family and not others. The family members not represented by the question may feel sided against. Circular questions that follow only one viewpoint for too long risk alienating family members and getting the therapist stuck in viewing family members or issues in only one way. Having a complex view of a goal and strengths allows for greater inclusion and an increased number of paths to success.

Circular questions are ideal for respecting a family's culture because the ideas introduced by a circular question are the statements of a family member. The therapist decides how to frame the ideas and transposes static characteristics into interactional terms, but the ideas are based upon the family's input.

A simple circular question takes a statement made by one member and asks other members if that is the way they view the issue, too.

THERAPIST: Meimei, you said that you enjoy family board games. (Turning to the other family members) What do y'all think of Meimei's idea for family togetherness? Playing family board games?

The circular question took Meimei's idea, accentuated it by repetition in a paraphrase, involved other family members in the process, and prompted each to contribute. Meimei's statement was helpful because it did not need to be transformed. Her goal-oriented idea already included others and suggested helpful interactions.

Systemic information presents the interconnections of people. Helpful solutions are stated in interactional descriptions. A final circular question addressed to all the family members could ask about the relevance of Meimei's idea in contributing to the family goal.

THERAPIST: So how is the family playing board games related to the family communicating more? How is that helpful?

With the introduction of the link between the solution and the goal the circular question acts as an intervention. The circular question also queries the members about whether indeed this idea does move them toward their goal from each person's perspective.

REFRAMING

Therapeutic reframing presents the family with an alternate viewpoint of what has become an established family "truth." For example, "Dad is too busy to play with me." "Nikki is a slob." "Davon is always angry." "Mom and Dad fight all the time." *Reframing* is an interpretation that describes some bit of data accurately but with a slight twist. It is meant to insert some new information for family review that could lead to more a more helpful understanding of a particular family "truth" or dynamic (Watzlawick et al., 1974; Weeks & L'Abate, 1979).

An effective, simple form of reframing occurs when paraphrasing the statements of a family member with the addition of a positive motive. Adding a positive motive to alter a prevailing and unhelpful interpretation may allow progress.

FATHER: This constant focus on cleaning and neatness around the house is driving us all away. We're afraid to drop a crumb or spill a drop because she'll zoom in with the vacuum or mop within 10 seconds.

THERAPIST: So one big thing Mom does with her time is to worry about having a nice place for all of you. Does she show her love for you guys in any other ways?

This reframing of mom's cleaning behavior moves the attribution from an unstated but clearly negative frame (perhaps compulsive or controlling?) to a just as "real" motive—that is, the positive attribution of love. Mom does it because of her commitment to the family's well-being. No one knows the reality of mom's motive, the real motive. The social construction makes a real motive. Mom may not know why she behaves in such a way. She is likely, however, to appreciate the attribution of love more than a negative attribution of a compulsive or controlling person. Her positive emotion of appreciation or pride (or whatever her positive feeling may be) will allow her to embrace change with more energy and creativity. Mom no longer needs to defend herself from the criticism of her moral failures. She can express her strength, love, in a different manner. Probability for change and sociability are increased in the family.

Research on reframing underscores its importance in psychotherapy (e.g., Conoley & Garber, 1985; Robbins, Alexander, Newell, & Turner, 1996) and the social influence literature (e.g., Davis & Knowles, 1999). Reframing may occur at any point in therapy, but it is often used early in the process of formulating family goals (Johnston, Levis, & L'Abate, 1986; Selvini-Palazzoli, Boscolo, Cecchin, & Prata, 1977).

Reframing can help parents expand their understanding of their children's troubling behavior. This difference can invite compassion rather than sanctions. A misbehaving child elicits parental anger. Often this anger maintains the very issue the parents wish to remedy (Fisch et al., 1982). For example, parents may be furious and embarrassed upon learning their daughter has engaged in shoplifting. Their fury interferes with their communication. And their embarrassment turns to intense worry about their daughter's future life of crime.

THERAPIST: Your daughter has done something wrong. She made a mistake. Unfortunately, most children make this mistake at some point in their development. I wonder what your daughter is searching for? Are there any sad or empty parts of her life?

Evoking compassion for a child's issues by reframing can make creating a positive goal easier because punitive feelings are lessened in the parents. In our culture, thieves are rehabilitated through punishment. Changing the child's problem into a child in search of something opens the gate to many more possible goals and strategies. A child being supervised because we want her to be happy and safe is treated with a very different emotional tone than would be available for a potential thief.

FATHER: Well I didn't know that most kids shoplift and that doesn't make it right. I don't care if every kid shoplifted. My LaVerne is better than that. I don't know what she might be looking for. Excitement, attention . . .. I don't know.

THERAPIST: I am impressed that even when you're upset you know how wonderful your child is—she's not like every other kid. Did you hear that, LaVerne? Your Dad thinks you are exceptional. I wonder if LaVerne is looking for excitement or acceptance from peers. How could we offer her other alternatives?

Frequently, family interactions are strained by angry outbursts from members. A therapist can suggest that behind displays of anger are often feelings of hurt or sadness (Greenberg & Goldman, 2008). Children's angry outbursts elicit angry responses or withdrawal by parents, but the idea of a sad child immediately elicits a different response from parents. "What is wrong with my child?" can be transformed into, "What can we do to make our child happier?" The point of reframing is not to deliver a better or truer slice of reality, but rather an interpretation that promotes a different response or initiates a different interaction. This difference could be the start of a new pattern that redirects the family toward its goals rather than keeps it stuck in unhappiness and nonproductive behaviors.

A child may express strong concerns that her mother nags her continuously. The label of nagging is harsh, usually leading into a familiar family argument (a dance of anger) of one accusation after another. However, reframing the statement can redirect the discussion into a more productive path.

THERAPIST: So you do not like the way your mother shows concern for you. How would you like her to show concern?

Moving into a goal orientation from a reframe changes the child's mindset. Asking about "concern" changes the focus from a negative process (nagging) to a positive process (concern). If the therapist merely followed the child's exact frame and language, the question would have been, "How do want your mom to nag you?" Framed in that way, the question would lead right into the old way of thinking, which has not been productive. If the old label worked, the family would not be bringing it up!

While acting-out behavior and anger are the number one concerns of parents who bring their children to family therapy, there are other concerns. A child who lacks empathy, is disengaged with the family, and is not warm could be reframed as a "thinker" rather than an uncaring and cold person. A thinker may need to develop greater feeling orientation to be successful with peers and adults. Parents may warm to the task of teaching a child about empathy or feelings with greater acceptance than they do dealing with their own feelings of rejection. Parents who are concerned that their child is lazy or passive may respond more positively to a frame of laid back, relaxed, mellow, or accepting. They can see some strength in being mellow that does not exist in being lazy. Neither of these examples suggests that parents accept the status quo presented by their children. Their jobs are to guide and teach their children according to their family values. The point of the reframe is to provide the parents with more creative energy to do their jobs.

Parents are, of course, also negatively labeled by their children and sometimes by each other. When parents negatively label each other about child raising issues, the accusations often point out that one is too harsh and the other too lenient. These descriptions conceptually parallel the enmeshed to disengaged continuum described by the founders of the Structural Family Therapy movement (Minuchin, 1974). Essentially, parents label each other as being too involved (usually with the children) or too distant (usually from the children and the other spouse). These characterizations may describe family functioning accurately, but labels do not lead the family to its goals.

FRUSTRATED FATHER, JOSE: Suzanna allows the children to do anything. She spoils them rotten. She sticks up for them no matter what they do and never makes them finish anything. They don't do chores and their grades are rotten!

THERAPIST: So you're frustrated with the situation. It sounds like you recognize that Suzanna is a kind, loving mother—which is a good thing. I imagine that you want her to continue being a kind, loving, and loyal person to you and the children. At the same time, you are worried that her kindness is lost on the children. Are they taking advantage of her kindness and developing habits that worry you? Do you need more influence with them?

JOSE: Suzanna is a great mother. She is forgiving and incredibly patient. But I think the kids treat her like a doormat and she needs to take a stand.

SUZANNA: He's never home and when he does get home he's busy and grumpy. Jose doesn't seem to understand or want to understand what kids need or how much time it takes to raise them. I do feel like a doormat sometimes . . . to everyone.

THERAPIST: Sounds like you are both frustrated with the situation and perhaps both feeling a bit ignored by the other. The good news seems to be that Dad wants influence with his children and thinks you are a great Mother. You agree that you are feeling somewhat taken advantage of and may be looking for an ally to help you move from doormat to doorway.

Once obtaining both perspectives on a family interaction, the summary can contain tandem perspectives that include both as important. Using both rather than one perspective is called *both/and logic* rather than *either/or logic*. Understanding how both (or more) perspectives contain important information enfranchises all and builds upon strengths.

THERAPIST: Suzanna, you want the children to enjoy learning so that they will be curious about knowledge and be life-long learners, constantly growing! And Jose, you want the children to be able to work hard at tasks even when the work is not enjoyable. You know that grades are important and that their future jobs are not always fun. Both of you have really important wisdom on this issue. How can the children learn from both of you?

Combining reframed perspectives and both/and presentations can be complex. The process is an advanced skill. Cleverly, Insoo Kim Berg and Steve DeShazer have recommended having a therapy break at the end of each session so that the therapist can review the session to devise such a presentation (Berg, 1994). They recommend linking the reframing *both/and* statement to a homework assignment that fits the issue. Further examples of this will be presented throughout the book.

A comment the therapist might make to the children could be:

THERAPIST: You guys have heard what your parents have said about you. They both have great dreams for you and think you have good potential.

They are both worried a little, however, about whether you guys know how great you can be. I wonder if we can explore how you show your parents your strengths as family members.

PARENT AS MODEL

Parents should view themselves as powerful models for and the most significant influences on their children. Emphasizing a parent's role as the primary model for a child occurs directly and indirectly in every session of therapy. Promoting this notion with parents underscores the respect the therapist has for the parents and so it contributes to rapport building. It says to parents that, although they have sought help from a therapist, the major changes experienced in therapy and beyond will come from their efforts. We view them as competent. Parents must feel responsible for and feel able to promote their children's welfare. In the same way that a therapist accepts the role of influencing the course of a session, parents must gain confidence that they have tools to influence the development of their children. Without this belief, a family flounders.

Therapists can ask about the parents' abilities, talents, and hobbies. It is important to have a comprehensive understanding of their strengths—even ones that are not entirely obvious to them or their children.

THERAPIST: One of the strengths I notice about you is that you have strong values. Which of your values do you think you are best at teaching through your behaviors?

Later in the course of therapy, parents can be asked about modeling communication skills.

THERAPIST: How can the family reach the goal of positive communication among all the members? Which two or three people in the family are doing the best at this right now? What are some of the details of good communication they are teaching everyone else?

When children are feeling and/or acting out of control, parents often resort to punishment as a way to regain control. The disappointment, frustration, and fear that parents feel at their children's difficulties are often expressed as anger. The hidden cost of anger and punishment is, however, withdrawal. All of us withdraw from punishing consequences and people. Most of us avoid angry individuals. While trying to increase influence, parents actually lose influence by a primary reliance on anger and punishment.

When punishment does not work, the parent reports feeling disrespected. Typically, children cannot communicate their experience clearly and certainly are rarely as articulate or analytical as the parent. This normal developmental difference between parents and children can lead to both parties feeling confused and more frustrated with each other. The social construction of reality in a family is more influenced by the most powerful and articulate. Children entangled in this kind of snare most often express the family problem as their feeling picked on or criticized too often.

The first goal, "stop being picked on," is not a good one because it merely reduces a problem. It can be shaped, however, from "not being picked on" to something like "having fun with mom every day." A goal of having fun with mom changes mom's meaning. She moves from a source of negativity to a source of fun. Transforming mom to a source of fun includes an important benefit: Mom becomes a role model and is listened to more carefully because we all tend to relate better to happier people. Researchers have determined that predictably stable families have a 5:1 positive to negative interaction ratio even during stressful periods (Gottman, 1994; Gottman & Levenson, 1999).

THERAPIST: How would you notice that you were not being picked on? What would be different? How would Mom talk with you? What would you do together when the picking stopped?

LaVERNE: Oh, I don't know. . . . She would smile at me and she would say that she liked my friends. I think if we were not fighting so much, we'd do more things together, but she'd also leave me alone when I needed to be alone.

THERAPIST: So when the picking stopped, your Mom would be noticing a lot of nice things about you, giving you some personal space, but also inviting your friends over sometimes because she liked them because you liked them. Do I have that right?

MOM: She is so angry so much of the time that I feel criticized and hopeless.

THERAPIST: Anger does that to us. What's curious is that LaVerne is missing your smiles and your attention and may need some help in organizing inviting a friend over. I think it's nice when kids need us.

THE MIRACLE QUESTION

The *miracle question* is a trademark intervention in Solution Focused Therapy (de Shazer et al., 2007). The therapist asks the clients to imagine that the problem(s) that brought them into therapy has/have disappeared magically. The therapist pursues the question by asking family members to report on how their lives would be different, after the miracle, in minute detail. Their reports describe the interactions of each person.

THERAPIST: What does your father say to you? What expression does he have on his face? How do you respond? What do you say? Are you smiling?

Responding to the miracle question allows family members to experience goal achievement. The follow-up questions require the family to identify with great precision how their interactions would be changed by the magical event. They are prompted to describe how they maintain the positive changes that occur because of the miracle. Their participation in this magical simulation introduces them to the exact interactions they must develop to reach their goals, but all the hard work is avoided. If done in detail, the miracle question leads to a visualization of the goal and its constituent parts. The process outlines with clarity what each person can do to contribute to success. The systemic nature of change is clarified during the process.

Steve de Shazer provides an excellent example of a miracle question. The question is asked with great drama and portent.

> Now, I want to ask you a strange question. Suppose that while you are sleeping tonight and the entire house is quiet, a miracle happens. The miracle is that the problem which brought you here is solved. However, because you are sleeping, you don't know that the miracle has happened. So, when you wake up tomorrow morning, what will be different that will tell that a miracle has happened and the problem which brought you here is solved? (de Shazer, 1988, p. 5).

de Shazer's initial and follow-up questions make the family problem or issue a product of the whole system because each person hears about or personally describes his or her own contribution to the new miracle life. Getting people to buy into a miracle is far easier than getting them to own a problem. With a greater understanding of the systemic nature of the solution, frustration can be reduced. The answer to reaching the family's goals does not rest upon one person's shoulders. Additionally, a clear realistic visualization of life without the problems and with most or all of the goals accomplished means that the individuals know how to accomplish their goals. The miracle question circumvents the issue of who will change first. They all can say what the simultaneous changes are in the new miracle life and they can experience hope.

Insoo Kim Berg demonstrates a miracle question while working with a couple in the videotape *Irreconcilable Differences* (1997). Her presentation is hypnotic. She sets the stage by clearly announcing that something different is about to happen. She shifts her body; her affect becomes brighter and pleasantly mischievous as if she is about to deliver a wonderful surprise. She asks in the introduction if the family believes in miracles. They say yes. She replies "Oh good." The family laughs with anticipation. If they said no, we suppose she would have said with a bright laugh, "Then you are really in for a treat!" She asks the miracle question and they laugh again.

After the laughter subsides from the miracle question, the follow-up questions are critical. While asking the questions, Berg illustrates how to use future tense confused with the present and presuppositional language. That is, the therapist must use language that assumes or supposes that the change occurred already or will certainly occur. For example, "What will be different now that the miracle happened?" "What will you do now?" "When you wake up tomorrow, how are you feeling?" There is no room for "if" or "try" in presuppositional language.

When using the miracle question, frequently bring the family back to the fantasized miracle description. Keeping within the new state will be difficult for most family members. Remind them of the miracle happening when they slip into an old interaction.

THERAPIST: Okay, that was the old days. Now that the miracle has happened, what are you doing tomorrow when Jim wakes up by himself with only one reminder!

The follow-up questions should lead the family members to clearly visualize the interactional or relational solution to reaching their goals. The systemic assumption is that each person can contribute to the family goals.

ENACTMENT

Just as the miracle question allows families an opportunity to gain experience through visualization or fantasy, enactment allows families the opportunity to experience growth or success through practicing in a session. Enactment occurs when the family members reproduce in session acts that have happened or they wish to have happen at home. Having the family enact (role play themselves) an important process or dynamic within the session allows us to coach their communication skills.

While enactment allows the family safe practice in the session, the process also serves as an assessment tool. Family members discover some of the roadblocks to their goals by trying out behaviors in session. Imagine that a family goal has been formulated: *The child will get out of the shower when asked one time and the parent will ask in polite and happy ways.* This can be enacted in the session. Parents may need coaching on "polite and happy." A child may need lots of reinforcement for even going through the motions of compliance. A therapist may have to provide enthusiastic reinforcement as a model to parents who may not know that establishing a new behavior takes some extra effort. With younger children, movement can be important. This is a great time for therapists to experience the thrill of producing and directing plays. These can be fun and set up to involve everyone. They are best done to practice the goal, not to invite a sociodrama of old patterns. The old, unhelpful patterns may certainly emerge and thereby be available for redirecting and coaching.

FINDING EXCEPTIONS

A family's goals most often contain elements that the family has partially or perhaps entirely accomplished in the past. The goal may be for greater consistency of producing the goal; they experienced some of their desired state and want more. An examination of past successes with even a part of a goal reveals client strengths. Any time a past or partial success is discovered, we say it is an *exception*. *Exceptions* (de Jong & Berg, 1998; de Shazer et al., 2007) are experiences that our clients had of their problems *not* occurring.

Exploring when the clients have experienced some success with their goals provides valuable insights into what strengths the clients have to jump-start and complete goal attainment. Asking carefully about the circumstances and details of the past partial successes provides building blocks to grow upon. Additionally, remembering abilities and past successes increases hope.

WIFE, SUZANNA: When we were first married and before the children came, we used to find the time to talk about each other's day. That felt good. I felt important.

HUSBAND, JOSE: Yeah, we'd take a walk or lie around in bed and sometimes talk or read the paper and talk about the stories. I guess we got too busy, but we . . .

THERAPIST (INTERRUPTING): So when you take a little time together it feels good. A walk or a talk seems to bring you closer. Is this feeling of closeness something that you want more of in your future? Can you think of how to find these moments right now?

SCALING QUESTIONS

Asking clients to gauge their experiences provides a simple way for complex issues to be communicated (Berg, 1994; Berg & de Shazer, 1993; Berg & Miller, 1992; de Shazer et al., 2007). *Scaling questions* provide a structure for clients to communicate their observations on a scale from zero to 10. Clients can rate, for example, their motivation to work toward their goal; their confidence that their goal will be achieved; the ranking of what their next best step toward the goal might be; or when termination from therapy should occur (De Jong & Berg, 1998).

Scaling how much effort each person is willing to exert to accomplish the goal gauges each member's motivation.

THERAPIST: How hard are you willing to work to accomplish this goal? If zero means you are not going to do one thing and ten means you are going to do everything possible, where are you?

The level of motivation reveals whether the goals are important to everyone. Additionally, asking about willingness to work to achieve a goal clearly indicates that each person must contribute and that change is not created by a magic spell or medicine that the therapist concocts or prescribes.

The timing of scaling questions bears some discussion. These questions are done best rather late in the therapy process. We cannot ask clients about family goals until we have worked to increase their understanding of what could be, their motivation to try, and their confidence that they can succeed. In other words, we should ask them to scale issues only that have reached some level of personal significance for them. The scaling questions can follow therapeutic strategies that lead to goal formulation and questions that explore exceptions. Having a family member say he or she intends to do nothing to accomplish a goal early in therapy can set the process back significantly.

A zero score is most often given by the children in a distressed family. Making certain that the goal includes the child's perspective is imperative to avoid a therapeutic detour. Once a child feels enfranchised, the level of work the child pronounces he or she will do often surprises everyone.

Gauging the amount of confidence family members have that their goals can be reached indicates faith in family therapy and their level of hope. Therapists should pay attention to the scaling and refocus conversations on goals, reframing, compliments, finding exceptions, and emphasizing approach motivation if the scaling is low. However a person answers a scaling question, we should be pleased that it is higher than we expected. This contributes to the positive emotions of the session and hope.

Our favorite scaling question measures a family's perceptions about the extent of goal attainment that they feel has been accomplished. Goals can be pictured as a series of stepping-stones. The ultimate goal may be easy to see, while the smaller steps are more intricate to describe. The scaling question allows clear communication about these steps. The questions are meant to move a person's perceptions up one unit on the scale of goal attainment at a time.

THERAPIST: So you rate that you are at a 4 now out of 10 steps to your goal. What would it take just to move a little toward 10? What would need to happen for you to think it was a 5?

The process communicates the importance of making progress in manageable steps. This increases confidence and allows for celebration along the way.

Gauging how far the person is along the continuum from zero to ten in reaching a goal also shares the multiple perspectives of each person as well as provides a chance to talk about therapy termination.

THERAPIST: Where are you now on the number scale of your goal for your parents to be happy with you? If zero is that your parents yell angrily every time they see you and ten is that your parents are happy every time they see you, what number tells us where are you now?

After making some progress on goals, the follow-up question to the goal-scaling question can address termination.

THERAPIST: How high do you need to be in order to continue being happy without seeing me? To stop family therapy?

This communicates that the ultimate goal does not have to be accomplished during family therapy and introduces the idea of termination.

CHAPTER CONCLUSION

These fundamental techniques form the basis of working with families. The Positive Family Therapy techniques involve and empower each family member in the design and construction of a new family reality. The family's strengths, which include the culture, talents, and enjoyed activities, form the foundation that supports family growth. The therapist must be accepted by and attuned to each member so that each contributes and benefits from the process. Many of the techniques of Positive Family Therapy are different from individual therapy techniques. Harm and wasted time are minimized by actively interrupting and structuring the process. The content focuses on the individuals' desired outcomes instead of what they want stopped. Statements that include a positive thought, behavior, or feeling are accentuated through restatement, deeper questioning, or involving other family members in the process. Negative thoughts, feelings, or behaviors are respectfully noted but not celebrated with attention, and, if untimely or repetitious, they are actively avoided. Goal-oriented actions are fantasized and enacted in the session. Each person has a role in the goal-oriented actions; each person benefits. Each person assesses the process and outcome. These are the basic technical skills of a Positive Family Therapist.

CHAPTER 3

Family Interventions Enriching
Positive Family Therapy

GOAL OF CHAPTER 3

In this chapter we describe interventions therapists assign for families to do as homework between sessions. To increase the families' success of implementing between-session practice, therapists must consider issues of treatment acceptability, in addition to treatment efficacy. Mastery of this material will assist therapists in developing a family's motivation to attempt and maintain homework assignments that promote family happiness.

Key Concepts in Chapter 3: acceptability, behavioral guidance, capitalization, catch them being good, collective cultures, coping model, emotional intelligence, empathy, Formula First Session Task, gratefulness, individualistic cultures, modeling, psychological guidance, rituals, routines, self-awareness, self-management, social awareness, social support, social skills, successive approximations.

OVERVIEW

Research and experience support the usefulness of many family interventions during therapy sessions. Many of these were described in the previous chapter. The family's work between the sessions is very important, however, as they build new skills for happy family life. Developing and assigning these tasks consists of a mix of applying available research and clinical artistry. The following pages focus on these between-session tasks with a strong focus on making it likely the family will do the homework.

ACCEPTABILITY

The most efficacious intervention is worthless if unused by clients. A paradox in all the helping professions is that people often do not do what is in their best interests. This includes not taking the medicine that is prescribed, eating healthy food, exercising, or avoiding risky behaviors such as substance abuse (Osterberg & Blaschke, 2005; Scheel, Hanson, & Razzhavaikina, 2004; Schmidt & Woolaway-Bickel, 2000).

Psychological treatment has suffered from similar problems with treatment compliance. For example, early behavioral psychologists experienced a rejection of their effective interventions apparently because teachers, parents, and others charged with implementing the strategies viewed the interventions as too harsh (Kazdin, 1981; Wolf, 1978). Kazdin noted that, although a treatment may resolve a presenting problem, it may be viewed as inappropriate, unfair, unreasonable, or too intrusive. If these perceptions exist, even successful strategies will be discontinued. Understanding how to increase treatment acceptability is an important research area and critical to practitioners. Having a good or even a perfect idea about how to enhance family process is not enough.

Kazdin's (1981) formulation of acceptability directs practitioners to investigate clients' perceptions about aspects of the treatment (e.g., how complex, how much time will it take, how disruptive is it to a daily routine) in order to maximize acceptability. For example, if the client sees the directive to use "negative reinforcement to extinguish an undesirable behavior," as impossible to carry out, Kazdin might suggest the clinician say, "Don't give him any dessert until he finishes his dinner."

Our own research into this vital area of clinical practice (e.g., Conoley, Conoley, Ivey, & Scheel, 1991) supports Kazdin's insights but has uncovered some needed expansions. In particular, our findings identify the relationship between the therapist and the clients as highly predictive of treatment use. Specifically, it seems important to make sure that:

1. The client sees a fit or connection between the therapeutic goal[1] and the intervention.
2. Clients believe the intervention is doable, effective, and matches their ethical/moral values.
3. The client-therapist relationship is strong.

---

1. In the original research we stated a problem but have since evolved.

Variations across these three dimensions of fit to goal, match to personal variables, and relationship with therapist cause changes in whether or not clients agree to attempt a therapeutic homework assignment.

Of course, agreement is a vital step, but implementation is imperative (i.e., talk is cheap). The key issue in implementation is ability. Has the family gotten enough direction to understand what is expected? Has the homework been enacted in a session so the family members have been coached to know what success looks like? Telling a family to "talk nicely to each other for one hour per day" is unlikely to work, especially if coercive processes are the norm among them. Therapists must give very specific directions. For example, in a family displaying negative communication between parents and an adolescent child about money, a therapist could suggest:

THERAPIST: When LaVerne asks for money, I want you to ask her about what she wants to buy and then be excited about the purchase. I want you to say, 'You have such good taste in shoes and look great in that color.' You may or may not be able to give her the money, but I want you to join in her excitement about shopping and help her make plans about how she might earn the money.

If an intervention is implemented, the ultimate goal is its continuous use, or *maintenance*, by the family. Intervention maintenance depends on three factors.

1. Did clients try the assignment—that is, did they implement it between sessions?
2. Did they experience it as enhancing positive affect or well-being?[2]
3. Was the change they experienced related to the intervention sufficiently powerful to move them toward their goals?

Although each of these points appear obvious, they are critical to the success of family therapy (e.g., Conoley, Padula, Payton, & Daniels, 1994; Conoley et al., 1991; Padula, Conoley, & Garbin, 1998; Scheel et al., 2004). Obviously, if a family reports they did not try the assignment (e.g., too busy, were too mad at each other, could not get cooperation), therapists have to return to increasing the acceptability of the suggestion (or some other intervention). If they tried it but it "didn't work," the therapist must

---

2. In the original model we stated *tolerable disruption*, but we have incorporated the research on the Build and Broaden Theory.

ask them to show what happened within the session so that family members can be coached. If they are doing the assignment, but doubt whether it is having a big enough effect, the therapist can add therapeutic elements and/or motivate them to persist (e.g., "Building a great family can't happen in just one week").

Many families enter therapy not knowing fully that reaching their goals requires real and permanent adjustments in how they all interact with each other. Medical practitioners report difficulty in motivating clients to take medication for 5 days (Osterberg & Blaschke, 2005). The problem of motivating and supporting individuals to make life-long changes is not trivial.

In one research project that examined the ability of the expanded acceptability model to predict assignment implementation, a 90% accuracy level was achieved (Conoley et al., 1994). Three acceptability variables are powerful predictors of homework completion.

1. Did the therapist present the intervention as matching and using the client's strengths? *Strengths* are anything clients say they enjoy doing or are good at doing.
2. Did the client see the match or the fit between the intervention and the client's understanding of the goal or problem? The assignment can be novel, but some rationale must be provided to the family that convinces them that it has a connection to what they care about.
3. Was the homework at an appropriate level of difficulty? Was it doable given the clients' understanding, time constraints, and assessed level of motivation?

In summary, if therapists question and listen, they can develop and present interventions in a manner that increases the likelihood of the client trying them. Importantly, assessing a family member's strength occurs simply through attending to whether the activity is enjoyed or is something the client is good at doing. Linking the intervention to incremental movement toward the family's goal, then asking if it makes sense, can assure that the intervention fits the family members' understanding of the goal and the intervention. A therapist will not be successful with a cookbook of interventions or assignments that are prescribed without attention to the open-system/meaning-making quality of families.

Assessing the client's experience of the difficulty level of the assignment can be accomplished while simultaneously investigating the possible roadblocks to its implementation. Asking the family to enact the intervention in the session uncovers problems that might derail a successful attempt.

Family members may not understand a therapist's directions or the family context may not be clear to the therapist. It is up to the therapist to investigate both their understanding and the situation they will face in practicing their homework. Asking the family to act out the intervention physically or play through a visualization of the intervention can expose roadblocks before they occur. An in-session enactment may warn the therapist away from assigning a particular strategy or allow some problem solving about contextual roadblocks. If the enactment suggests the family is not ready, a therapist can say:

THERAPIST: What you just tried is a very advanced skill. When you are a little closer to reaching your goals, this will be easier. For now, let's try something else that is a better match to what your next step needs to be.

It is common for family members to dispute the relationship of the assignment to their goal because they may still be holding on to the notion that the end point of therapy is merely getting rid of the problem that brought them to counseling. The therapist must be agile in providing reasonable rationales to explain why implementing a new interactional pattern will help them as a family.

THERAPIST: You guys have done a whole lot of things that have worked for your family in the past. Right now, however, its time is to do something that is brand new—something that you're good at, but have not been doing. This new idea will open up some creative alternatives that have been lost because you've been so stressed.

Attending to the details of making a suggested intervention acceptable to clients is well worth the effort.

FORMULA FIRST SESSION TASK

Steve de Shazer (1984, 1985) describes a first session homework assignment that is meant to benefit clients by helping them clarify their goals, become more optimistic about achieving their goals, and increase their cooperation in therapy. This intervention, the *formula first session task* (FFST), is summed up by the following therapist direction:

> Between now and the next time we meet, we would like you to observe, so that you can describe to us next time, what happens in your family that you want to continue to have happen. (de Shazer, 1985, p. 137)

The FFST compares favorably to other problem-focused first session homework assignments. When comparing the FFST to a standard problem-focused structural-strategic intervention, the FFST intervention had higher compliance, clarity of treatment goals, and improvement in the presenting problem (Adams, Piercy, & Jurich, 1991).

This intervention is especially useful when the family cannot converge on goals endorsed by all the members. Notice that each member is asked to find something about the family that should continue, something that is working. They are asked to attend to the positives of their family at a time when they are consumed with thoughts about what is going wrong. Extensive research about how people process information supports the power of *selective attention*. Further, research from positive psychology underscores the power of focusing on *blessings* (Emmons & McCullough, 2003). People who spend time thinking about good things (e.g., what they are grateful for) get happier. Happier people think more clearly, have more energy, and come up with more creative solutions to problems (Lyubomirsky, King, & Diener, 2005).

Predictably, therefore, after the family members implement the FFST assignment, their goal orientation increases and they become more present- than past-focused. Because blame and failure are associated with the past, moving to the present and future is a very helpful therapeutic shift.

The other benefit of the FFST intervention is the uncovering of family members' strengths. What the members identify as things they appreciate become the building blocks of further interventions because these experiences are targeted for expansion and maintenance. Family members enjoy hearing from each other about strengths and so the reporting of the assignments contributes to confidence, hope, and pace of change.

This assignment sets the stage for the *exception* technique (de Shazer, 1985) described in Chapter 2. Each family member brings strengths to family therapy that will be used to move the family toward individual and shared goals. Often, they forgot these strengths or feel so troubled by their current concerns that they fail to attend to current examples of their historical strengths. The FFST begins a process of their uncovering exceptions to their problem—even the most troubling member of the family does something that promotes family welfare (e.g., Conoley et al., 2003; Dahl, Bathel, & Carreon, 2000).

The FFST is particularly helpful also because the assignment can fit any situation; therefore, the outcome of the first session feels more encouraging to family members. That is, even at a very early point in therapy, they have something new to do that is likely to surprise them. Further, assigning homework in the first session sets the norm for the rest of therapy. When therapy is going well, the most important work will be done between sessions. The FFST is easy to do and provides the family (and therapist!) with an early success. Success breeds hope, which predicts change.

FAMILY RITUALS

Family rituals are predictable acts that communicate the family's identity and values. Rituals form bonds that hold a family together and communicate a connection that lasts into future generations (Bossard & Boll, 1950; Moss & Moss, 1988; Troll, 1988). Asking a family about their rituals yields rich information about the family's identity. In reviewing 50 years of research on rituals, Fiese and her colleagues (2002) found that routines and rituals enhance families in many ways. Children are better behaved and healthier when they have functioning rituals. Children have increased resiliency to the risks associated with parental divorce, death in the family, single parenting, and remarried families when rituals continue. Family rituals can help children of alcoholics resist becoming problematic drinkers, thus interrupting the generational transmission of alcoholism (Wolin, Bennett, & Noonan, 1979; Wolin, Bennett, Noonan, & Teitelbaum, 1980).

Rituals benefit family members at all stages of life. Families with an infant or preschool child reported higher marital satisfaction when their rituals were meaningful (Fiese, Hooker, Kotary, & Schwagler, 1993). Families with meaningful rituals have children who are less anxious (Markson & Fiese, 2000). Adolescents from ritual-rich homes are less likely to drink alcohol (Fiese, 1993) and have higher psychological health and indexes of social development (Bomar & Sabatelli, 1996; Gavazzi, Goettler, Solomon, & McKenry, 1994; Gavazzi & Sabatelli, 1990).

Common family rituals are celebrations of birthdays, anniversaries, religious holidays, secular holidays, reunions, weddings, and funerals. They include predictable happenings such as attending religious services, Sabbath meals, and Sunday dinners.

Rituals are more than family routines, but they are built from routines. Typical family routines are associated with dinnertime, bedtime, chores, and regular telephone visits with relatives. Routines are habitual behaviors for getting something accomplished. Routines make family life easier because routines provide a predictable, almost automatic, process that feels secure to children and removes some of the effortful decision-making process from the parents. A routine, however, does not involve the symbolic meaning that is the heart of rituals. Rituals convey information about the identity of a family from generation to generation. Good feelings can be recaptured when a family member remembers the enactment of a family ritual. Therapists should remember, however, that routines can become rituals if they are given a symbolic meaning of significance to the family members. Consider the following exchange during which the therapist is both reinforcing an enjoyable family routine (i.e., bedtime story) and attempting to elevate it to a time devoted to the transmission of important family information and values.

THERAPIST: You always read a story to your children before bed. Is that a pleasant time for everyone?

MOTHER: I do like it and the kids seem to like the time as well. We sit together on the bed and cuddle. That feels good.

THERAPIST: So nightly story time is a time you connect with your kids physically and a chance to communicate some important values through what you choose to read because you know you have their attention.

MOTHER: I hadn't thought of the values part. I've just been picking up any book that was around. I do have some books on relating to grandparents and cousins that might be good to go over. We're so far away from each other, I'd like them to remember they are part of a bigger family.

Rituals are a window into the family's identity and strengths (Imber-Black, Roberts, & Whiting, 1988; Wolin & Bennett, 1984). They are a unique element in the progress of a family to keep what is valuable about the family while evolving to meet individual needs and changing times. Children and adolescents rarely appreciate all family rituals. Parents, in the face of the children's resistance, may capitulate and cease certain celebrations or patterns. For example, many families have abandoned shared family meals in service to busy schedules of both parents and children. Some report their common dinnertime is often in a car on the way to a child's lesson.

What is lost in this modern, car-culture, hurried-child meal plan is more than healthy food (Videon & Manning, 2003). Families need arenas in which to practice social support, transmission of values, appreciation of successes, analysis of problems, and establishment of norms—even time to teach table manners. Research has linked frequent (5–7 times per week) shared family meals to several positive family outcomes such as better nutrition, higher grades, and lower prevalence of eating disorders, substance use, depression, and suicide attempts (Eisenberg, Olson, Neumark-Sztainer, Story, & Bearinger, 2004).

Of course, family meals could also be interpersonal disasters if members used the time to belittle each other or resurrect time-worn complaints. The family meal is not a silver bullet of mental health, but regular time together as a family that is connected to feelings of safety, nourishment, sharing, and fun can be a very powerful ritual. If troubled families can start to add small positive experiences, the small changes can escalate. This process is not magical, but rather incremental as they broaden and build their repertoire of positive interactions and affect. Some of the interventions that follow can be understood and presented as new rituals the family may wish to embrace as their own.

INCREASING GRATITUDE

Gratitude is defined as a positive emotion associated with the belief that we received something of value. Emmons describes gratitude as a "felt sense of wonder, thankfulness and appreciation for life" (Emmons & Shelton, 2002, p. 459).

Grateful feelings lead to a plethora of good outcomes (McCullough, Emmons, & Tsang, 2002). Wood, Joseph, and Linley (2007) consider gratitude the parent of all virtues and Lyubomirsky (2008) identifies gratitude as a metastrategy for achieving happiness. She summarizes research illustrating the relationship of gratitude to increases in subjective well-being and social functioning and decreases in depression (Emmons & McCullough, 2003; Lyubomirsky, Sheldon, & Schkade, 2005; McCullough, Emmons, & Tsang, 2002; McCullough, Tsang, & Emmons, 2004; Seligman, Steen, Park, & Peterson, 2005; Watkins, 2004; Wood, Joseph, & Linley, 2007).

Expressing gratitude to a benefactor leads the benefactor to provide future benefits and aid (Bartlett & DeSteno, 2006; Carey, Clicque, Leighton, & Milton, 1976; McCullough, Kilpatrick, Emmons, & Larson, 2001; Rind & Bordia, 1995; Tsang, 2006). Thus, expressing gratitude enhances the resources that are available to individuals and families. Frequent expressions of gratitude build skills that are useful in creating supportive friendship patterns for children and adults.

In addition to friendship outside the family, gratitude facilitates family members having more positive thoughts about each other (Wood, Joseph, & Maltby, 2008; Wood, Maltby, Stewart, Linley, & Joseph, 2008). Parents eagerly endorse the virtue of gratitude—especially for the children. Many children receive continuous reminders to say "thank you" as a sign of gratitude. Emmons and Shelton's (2002) description of wonder and appreciation for life clearly is the zenith of gratitude. Little bits of wonder count as well, however. Families can experience gratitude everyday by noticing benefits, perceiving them as valuable, and savoring the experience.

Consistent with previous discussions on constructivism, the story clients tell themselves about events predicts whether or not they will be grateful

(Lakey, McCabe, Fisicaro, & Drew, 1996). A wife may not be grateful for a diamond birthday gift if it is judged unworthy (e.g., smaller than one received by a friend) or if she had to remind her husband of her birthday (Lane & Anderson, 1976; Okamoto & Robinson, 1997; Tesser, Gatewood, & Driver, 1968; Weiner, Russell, & Lerman, 1978, 1979). Children can be products of such privilege that they do not value or show gratitude for presents or favors. They may have received so much that their personal story reflects entitlement. Only increasingly grand benefits get attention when children feel they deserve a continuous supply of gifts. Called *adaptation* or the *hedonic treadmill* by positive psychology researchers (e.g., Brickman, Coates, & Janoff-Bulman, 1978), parents experience ingratitude from children who become increasingly demanding and less thankful the more they are given.

A seemingly simple intervention can make a big difference in children's experience of gratitude. A gratitude intervention called *counting your blessings* increased early adolescents' subjective well-being and optimism while decreasing their negative affect (Froh, Sefick, & Emmons, 2008). The adolescents were asked to list up to five things they were grateful for in the past day. This can be modified for family therapy by asking children to do the following everyday between sessions. Froh, Sefick, and Emmons's directions were:

> There are many things in our lives, both large and small, that we might be grateful about. Think back over the past day and write down on the lines below up to five things in your life that you are grateful or thankful for (p. 220).

These 11- to 13-year-old students followed the assignment daily for 2 weeks. After the intervention and at the 3-week follow up the students who practiced being grateful reported greater satisfaction with their school and higher well-being than did the control groups. The well-being scores increased further at the 3-week follow up. The increase of well-being over time fits with Fredrickson's (1998) broaden and build theory that predicts the increase in positive emotions leads to increases in our thought-action repertoires, which starts the cycle of positive emotions again, thus escalating the benefits of positive emotions.

Designing a family gratitude intervention demands attention to several dimensions. The central ingredients are asking family members to notice and appreciate or savor beneficial occurrences regularly. It is important to keep enough variety or enjoyment in the process so it stays emotionally involving. Memorized statements repeated over and over again without thought will not help.

Building the gratitude intervention into existing family's routines or rituals increases the chances of success. Using spiritual/religious traditions, if present, is a good idea because gratitude seems to be an important construct in religious traditions of many different types. For example, the therapist can ask a family to add a grateful ritual to their meal times. The rationale for doing this is to increase family members' well-being, help them have more friends, enjoy and value each other more, and be healthier and less anxious. The therapist can say:

THERAPIST: I'm going to ask you to do something very small that can have a lot of positive outcomes. You may not even believe that it can improve your family, but if you really try it, I hope you will be surprised at its power to enhance your family life.

Before doing the exact assignment, ask each person about the virtue of gratitude. Do they enjoy being thanked and noticed for good deeds? Do they offer gratitude to others? Do they recognize that gratitude is a very important human virtue? The idea of increasing gratitude is normally a pretty easy "sell." After getting interest from the members, the therapist suggests the general idea that a time devoted to noticing family blessings will enhance the family. Family members are then asked to personalize the idea to match it to their routines or rituals.

Religious families may like the notion of a prayerful discussion of thankful interactions with others or natural gifts noticed that day. Turns could be taken choosing a category of benefits to be noticed. The family could be appreciative of people who did something nice for them today or thankful they saw one of their favorite animals. Or elementary school-aged children might be asked to list newly mastered spelling words. These words could be enjoyable prompts for every other family member to associate with a blessing.

CHILD: I am grateful that I learned to spell three new words this week. The words are *Europe, ocean,* and *mountain.*
OLDER SISTER: I am grateful for the family trips we've taken to see the *mountains* and the *ocean* and hope that someday we might get to *Europe.*

The positive effects of gratitude depend on savoring the experience. Parents can play a powerful role in noticing and praising the statements of other family members and keeping a focus on the conversation. Slowing the process down and modeling involvement helps the children's engagement and likelihood of savoring the moments. Automatic and superficial routines are not helpful.

Families without religious traditions (e.g., those who do not say "grace" before meals) can still create family routines that focus on gratitude. We often ask family members to offer two compliments to each other family member, everyday. We have them practice in session giving and receiving compliments. Practice is important because many families have fallen out of the habit of saying nice things to each other. Take for example this recent attempt by a father to give his teenage daughter a compliment and the needed therapist follow up.

FATHER: You have such a beautiful smile and it makes me so happy to see you happy. I wish you would just smile more often, I hardly ever see that beautiful smile.

THERAPIST: The first part of what you said was a great compliment. She does have a lovely smile. What you said was like a verbal kiss. The second part, however, was a criticism, so you took away the kiss by giving a kick. Can you just give a kiss for now?

Families may need help in identifying what to compliment others about or what to appreciate that they receive. A dynamic in unhappy families is that they have stopped noticing the good things that surround them. Their attention has been narrowed to their problems. Reminding them of the gifts of life, good weather, available food, extended family, jobs, travels, past successes, small victories, their connection as a family, and so on may be necessary. A gifted teacher we know ends each day by complimenting his students as they leave his classroom. After a particularly tough day with a particular child we heard him say, "I think your braces are really working, Teddy. Your teeth look straighter to me." Now that's an adult who has mastered the skill of finding blessings!

If the therapist reminds family members about their own descriptions of present or past enjoyable activities, the details can initiate the process.

THERAPIST: I know you all are having some tough times, but I also recall that you may be grateful for those moments you share as a family when you go to the movies. Each of you mentioned fun times seeing blockbusters last summer. I wonder if you enjoyed this because you were grateful for your parents paying for it, for the great tastes of popcorn and soda, for the interesting conversations that followed about the movies, or for the time just to be laughing together.

SOCIAL SUPPORT

Social support is the experience of being loved, valued, and a part of a network of mutual obligation (Taylor, 2003). The network comprises family, friends, community organizations, and even pets. The experience of support can be emotional or about tangible assistance. Families provide emotional support via caring messages, responsive listening, and simply being present and loyal during good and hard times. Tangible assistance includes teaching, modeling, and financial and other material support.

Close relationships are central to human well-being (Diener & Oishi, 2005). Relationships keep stress levels down and immunological system functioning strong (Uchino, Cacioppo, & Kiecolt-Glazer, 1996). For example, Cohen and colleagues (1997) found that individuals with more diverse social networks (i.e., relationships from a variety of domains such as work, home, church) were less likely to develop clinical colds following inoculation.

The power of social support has been studied in many U.S. ethnic groups and different family structures with fairly consistent results. Both collective and individualistic cultures value and benefit from close relationships (Oishi, 2002; Diener, Oishi, & Lucas, 2003). Social support may be expressed differently, however, in well-functioning families across ethnic groups and acculturation experiences (e.g., Chao, 1994, 2001; Zayas, 1992). For example, although emotional closeness in Latino, African American, European American, and Asian families reduces the incidence of child abuse (Chao, 1994; Coohey, 2001; Mammen, Kolko, & Pilkonis, 2003; Medora, Wilson, & Larson, 2001), closer relationships between the parent and child in European American, but not first-generation Chinese American families (Chao, 2001), predict higher functioning children. More acculturated, second-generation Chinese American families, however, become similar to the European Americans on this variable.

A study of Latino families found that having one emotionally close parent to a middle school-aged boy or girl counters the negative effects of a conflictual relationship the child has with the other parent (Crean, 2008). A mother-daughter conflict could not, however, be balanced by a good father-daughter relationship. The mother-daughter relationship in a Latino home needs direct intervention to avoid negative effects for the girl.

Social support counters the stress of acculturation felt by recent immigrant families (Safdar, Lay, & Struthers, 2003; Thomas & Choi, 2006; Yeh & Inose, 2003). In fact, helping families connect with families of similar ethnic heritage and families from the majority culture can help immigrants' subjective well-being by promoting their bicultural identity development (Yoon, Lee, & Goh, 2008). *Bicultural identity* refers to the family's ability to value both their own heritage and the new host culture with success.

Dual career couples are a widespread family structure in the twenty-first century. A stress these couples experience is the overlapping and competing demands of work and family. These burdens can lead to exhaustion, diminished sexual intimacy, and recriminations about equitable family contributions. Partners' well-being is higher when each feels mutually supported (Parasuraman, Greenhaus, & Granrose, 1992). With higher mutual support between the partners, work-family conflicts and stress diminish (Adams, King, & King, 1996; Carlson & Perrewe, 1999; Parasuraman, Purhoit, Godshalk, & Buetell, 1996). The reduction in stress improves many relationship variables (Fensalson & Beehr, 1994).

Parental support may be expressed by careful identification and enactment of shared roles in child rearing, home maintenance, and extended-family obligations. Therapists should suggest that each member of a couple must give 100% (not 50%) for family success and that each partner must ask for what he or she needs. Mind reading is a poor substitute for direct conversation.

The hassles of child rearing strain almost every family. Special challenges confront dual career couples' coping repertoires. It is common for partners to revert to family-of-origin patterns when under stress (i.e., parent or expect others to parent as they were parented). This tendency can result in the couple adopting anachronistic behaviors that do not match their family goals. Who leaves work when the baby is sick? Who gets up at night to feed the baby? Who fixes the meals and cleans the house? Who manages communication with grandparents? Who handles the parent-teacher conferences or monitors the homework or settles the sibling disputes? The endless list of parental tasks requires full, close cooperation and support between the parenting partners to mitigate the predictable difficulties associated with growing families.

THERAPIST: You guys have a chance to build a unique partnership in raising your kids that takes the best from both of your experiences in your own families. What would be ideal? How could each of you feel important and special to the other?

Therapists are sometimes surprised at the small tokens that can communicate acceptable levels of social support. In response to the above therapist's statement, a young father said:

CLIENT: I wish Ellen would tell me once in a while that she thinks I'm doing a good job feeding or changing the baby. She always seems so anxious, like I'm going to make a mistake, that I am not sure if I'm really helping.

Families are the training ground for children's relationship skills with siblings, parents, and friends. A common relationship-enhancing, between-session assignment is to ask the family to play a game with each other before the next session. Game playing can grow cooperative skills and give practice in appropriate levels of competition. Along with promoting family fun, letting children see how to win and lose gracefully is the central goal of a game-playing assignment. Learning new games gives the parents or children practice in teaching and modeling skills. Parents can also show patience and tolerance for less-than-perfect performance.

Encouraging children to invite friends over is another strategy to teach children how to build social support networks. One family reported dismay that every play date disintegrated into arguments as their son insisted that his visitors play only the games he wished to play and to the level of expertise only he possessed. The family was fearful that he would never have close friends.

THERAPIST: What do you think is most important, the game or the person?
SON: The person is more important than the game.
THERAPIST: Why do you think the person is more important than the game?
SON: Well, with no people, I have no one to play with and people are just more important than games because there are a lot of games but each person is the only person like that.
THERAPIST: I think that's a terrific answer. You know that it's important to have friends for at least two reasons. One, people are unique and two, without people it's not much fun. How will you show your friends that they are important to you, even more important than some part of a game?
SON: I could thank them for coming over and I could let them make mistakes playing the games. That way they would have more fun and want to be around for more game playing.

This child improved his relationship skills both by being reinforced for this insight and by a nonverbal signaling program his parents and he established to use when he was entertaining friends. When he acted impatient with friends, his mother or father would signal him with a "thumbs down," indicating that he was reducing his friends' feelings of importance. When they noticed his patience or his encouragement toward friends they gave him a "thumbs up." This simple procedure helped him reach his goal of having a regular group of friends available for games.

Another strategy to enhance children's relationship skills is to connect them with extended family or with nonfamily-member adults. At times, an aunt, uncle, or family friend is a more influential model for a child than are the parents. Parents may need the therapist's intervention to appreciate this fact. They may feel rejected or competitive with the other adult. Reminding parents of all the good outcomes associated with social support, especially the effects of good adult-child relationships, may be helpful. In fact, it does "take a village to raise a child" and so parents can be grateful for and seek out assistance in managing the tasks.

If carefully chosen, talented baby sitters, tutors, or peer groups can also be part of the village. These individuals are often closer to children's ages than extended family members and family friends and may have even greater influence with a young person seeking models of action (see discussion of modeling later in this chapter). Models of the same or similar age and sex as children and whom children view as similar in competence may teach children skills and promote their self-efficacy for learning skills (Davidson & Smith, 1982). Schunk and Hanson (1985) found that children who observed a same-sex peer (student) solve difficult subtraction problems developed higher self-efficacy for learning to subtract than did children who observed a teacher solve the same problems. Instead of leaving a potent influence to chance, parents should purposefully involve helpful peer groups for their children.

CREATING CLOSENESS

Increased interpersonal closeness is often expressed as a family goal. Closeness among family members or friends can be achieved in many ways. The usefulness of rituals and compliments has been mentioned already. Another closeness-enhancing skill is *capitalization. Capitalization* means sharing positive events about self and celebrating others' successes (Langston, 1994). Sharing a positive event with someone, who responds actively and constructively, multiplies the benefits of a triumph. The family member enjoys the victory, the telling of the achievement, and the support received about the accomplishment (Gable et al., 2004). The research demonstrating the positive results of sharing everyday pleasant events is impressive. Sharing small pleasant events with a person who capitalizes upon them can counter depressive symptoms (Nezlek & Gable, 2001; Zautra, Schultz, & Reich, 2000). Self-esteem is enhanced by mutual celebrations of positive events (Beach & Tesser, 1995; Nezlek & Gable, 2001;

Tesser, Millar, & Moore, 1988). The key to success in capitalization is an affirming and enthusiastic response to the shared event. This positive intensity promotes more sharing and additional positive interpersonal processes (Gable et al., 2004).

Practicing capitalization in the session will help family members learn how to respond to the sharing of positive events with active, constructive responses that facilitate closeness and well-being. For example:

THERAPIST: I come home and tell you that I've just gotten a promotion. I say I'm happy and a little scared. What do you say?

CLIENT: I say, 'Don't worry because if it doesn't work out you still won't lose your job.'

THERAPIST: Okay. I can see you are picking up on the worry. Good, but I want you to capitalize on the promotion by saying something like, 'That is terrific news. You so deserve this promotion and you are so ready to be a star.' Can you try that?

Family members should be assigned the task of using affirming responses at home everyday. Of course, this also means that each family member must share a positive event, which incorporates the benefit-finding component of the gratefulness exercise as well. Also, the family members will need to be attending or focusing their attention upon what the family member is saying positively about her or himself. This process creates a positive focus as well. Be aware, however, that using capitalization will not be a natural skill for many members of a family. Research and clinical reports suggest that many men and women use active or passive destructive responses when confronted by good news. This means they tend to find the lurking dangers in every happy occurrence or they don't seem to care or pay attention to success (Gable et al., 2004). Both types of responses are destructive for the person sharing the good news even if the listener's intentions might be positive or neutral. The active destructive type may want to alert the person to unnoticed dangers—that is, be the devil's advocate for the family. Although there may be a place for skepticism or pessimism in certain circumstances, neither are positive family interventions. Both are common patterns, however, that may need disruption prior to assigning between-session capitalization tasks.

Similar benefits can be derived from family expressions of mutual caring through direct statements such as "I love you" or "I can't wait to see you" or "I'm thinking about you and missing you." Direct statements of caring are more or less common in different family cultures, but saying loving things apparently does no harm and may increase closeness of family members. In our clinical work, we have never heard complaints about too many sincere, loving statements, but we have often heard painful reports of feeling unloved, unnoticed, or dismissed by others.

These loving statements can be based on characteristics that family members value about each other. For example, parents should be encouraged to focus on the goals they have for their children in terms of virtues. The virtues they value may include kindness, honesty, reliability, persistence, altruism, obedience, flexibility, and so on. An important attentional skill for parents to develop is commenting on approximations of the target virtue. Similar to what is described later in the chapter as "catching them being good," reacting with loving and supportive statements to *successive approximations* is a tool that builds closeness while teaching virtues. Noticing successive approximations or incremental progress toward the goal makes further progress likely while rewarding the current attempt. The compliment should contain the behavior, attitude, or feeling that was noticed and the accompanying virtue. Coupling the virtue to the compliment is extremely important because the child will begin to define him/herself with the virtue. For example, "Juan, I really like the way you smiled at Jim. You are so friendly and kind!"

Parents and the therapist should not deny reality about an issue with a child in order to deliver a compliment. If a child complains about being overweight, the first response should not be to deny the belief. This is an ideal time to practice effective active coping strategies. Weight loss is on the minds of children and adults a lot these days, bringing with it inherent dangers.

MOM: You know Brittany, you don't seem overweight to me at all. Lets find out what the scientific charts say! Then we can see what is best for you.

BRITTANY: Okay, we can look it up on the computer! . . . (Later) See, Mom, I'm five pounds overweight.

MOM: All right, I don't think that five pounds is very much to worry about, but if you want to change that, we can figure out what to do. Okay? It is fun to set goals, figure out how to achieve them, and then celebrate success! But, first, why do you want to lose weight?

The discussion of what will be accomplished by a dubious cultural norm of losing weight to become more accepted or attractive needs to be discussed. In our example, mom accepts the goal of weight loss but states her goal is that she will diet and exercise too because it will make them both more healthy.

Helping a child accomplish a difficult goal, or more importantly enjoy working toward an impossible goal, can assist a child in many ways.

Viewing a parent as a source of endless support and willingness to be involved in a process toward a goal communicates many important messages. A parent delivering unbelievable positive platitudes does not continue to be a source of trusted help to a child.

BUILDING EMOTIONAL INTELLIGENCE

Emotional intelligence is a person's "ability to recognize, understand and use emotional information about oneself or others that leads to or causes effective or superior performance" (Goleman, 1995, p. 5). Emotional intelligence contributes to a wide range of benefits through the combination of cognitive reasoning and emotional sensitivity. High levels of emotional intelligence include well-developed self-awareness, self-management, social awareness, and social skills (Boyatzis, Goleman, & Rhee, 2000). *Self-awareness* refers to an accurate assessment of personal feelings, preferences, resources, and intuitions. *Self-management* is the ability to manage feelings, thoughts, and actions. *Social awareness* describes the ability to sense the feelings, needs, and concerns of others. *Social skills* are a constellation of abilities to communicate effectively and elicit desired response from others.

Connections between emotional intelligence and positive family life have been illustrated by a number of research studies. For example, higher emotional functioning can lead to educational success and personal development (Zins, Weissberg, Wang, & Walberg, 2004), career effectiveness (Mayer, Salovey, & Caruso, 2000; Mayer & Davidson, 2000), avoidance of drug problems (Trinidad, Unger, Chou, & Johnson, 2004), and increased skills in leadership and cooperation (e.g., Abraham, 2005; Daus & Ashkanasy, 2005). Overall, increasing emotional intelligence has been associated with better mental health, enhanced academic performance, and remediation of various behavior problems (Greenberg et al., 2003).

The constituents of emotional intelligence, self-awareness, self-management, social awareness, and social skills are all possible targets for family interventions. The concepts are not completely differentiated from each other and so do not suggest discrete interventions. But each element is suggestive of useful between-session assignments, depending on the family's strengths.

SELF-AWARENESS

Families can promote children's self-awareness by helping children notice and label feelings. Parents should ask their children how they feel about issues or circumstances and respond to expressions of feeling with empathy. The questions can be as simple as asking about children's experience of foods or as complex as asking them about their analysis of a movie or a current event. Dinnertime conversations that review the school day should include feeling statements. Helping the children with the vocabulary of feelings is important so children develop nuanced ways in which to express and experience the world of emotions. Parents can model sharing their day. Parents should be aware that the attitudes and feelings they reveal about work and friends will color the children's attitudes as well. Parents that report satisfaction and exciting levels of challenge associated with their work tend to promote similar attitudes in their children.

The most common mistake parents make in promoting self-awareness in children is that they use judgmental responses to children's feeling statements.

CHILD: I was angry today because I didn't get 100 on my spelling test. I studied hard and should have gotten everything right.

PARENT: Well, it's pretty stupid to be angry about that. Just study harder next time and you will get 100.

A better parental response aimed at promoting self-awareness in the child would be:

PARENT: I'm sorry you didn't get the grade you wanted. At whom are you angry? Are you angry at yourself or at someone else?

Before assigning self-awareness homework, therapists should do some teaching and some modeling. Everyone in the family has to practice accepting rather than disputing each other's feelings. There are no wrong feelings, although there are feelings that are unlikely to move people toward their goals. Parents may need practice in saying the following.

PARENT: It's okay to hate me, but it's not okay to hit me. And I want you to know that no matter what you feel, I love you now and forever.

Or the following.

PARENT: You say that you are stupid and I feel terrible that you doubt yourself like that. I can give you 100 examples right now why I think you are a very smart person.

Or the following.

PARENT: Now that you've stopped talking to your best friend, I wonder who is hurting. Is it you, or her? Does your decision to withdraw from her get you what you want? Are there other alternatives to deal with how disappointed you are in her?

SELF-MANAGEMENT/EMOTIONAL REGULATION

Helping family members learn to manage their behaviors and feelings is essential. Building self-management skills is a life-long process that may begin with toileting and continue through old age as individuals gain control over their behavior in the face of competing demands from internal and external sources. Routinely making prosocial decisions is a significant achievement. Describing some of their own challenges helps parents inspire children who, for example, refuse to get up on time.

PARENT: On the inside I was feeling a little lazy and wanted to just sleep, but then I realized that people at work were depending on me, so I got up on time. I want you to think about other people when it's time to get up, too.

Or parents can do the same with a child who has said hurtful things.

PARENT: It's okay to feel hurt when your sister criticizes you, but it's not okay to say mean things back. You can't take your mean words away once they are said. Think before you speak.

The ability to manage feelings allows for their effective and acceptable expression. This, in turn, earns greater influence with and support from others (Eisenberg, Fabes, Guthrie, & Reiser, 2000). Focusing attention on and away from feelings is the key to self-management (Eisenberg, Champion, & Ma, 2004; Eisenberg, Smith, Sadovsky, & Spinrad, 2004). Feelings are accentuated when people concentrate on them and continue to invest energy into keeping them in focus (i.e., rumination). In contrast, the skill of shifting attention away from negative thoughts (e.g., past negative feelings or experiences) to positive thoughts (e.g., benefit finding) reduces the power of negative thoughts and leads to additional positive feelings. Learning to purposefully manage positive and negative feelings allows family members to feel more confident in experiencing emotions. Feelings are not scary if they can be influenced effectively.

Skilled parents help children learn to shift emotional focus by using distraction as a tactic to increase acceptable behavior. When a child is involved in an unacceptable or dangerous activity, parents' first impulse is to say "No" or "Stop that!" A better response is to offer the child another activity that distracts him or her from the unwanted behavior. This is a more effective approach for at least two reasons.

1. It keeps the child from learning to say "No" and "Stop that!" continuously to the parent.
2. The technique demonstrates that self-management is facilitated by having an alternative activity or thought to occupy attention. As a child begins to understand the power of distraction, a powerful self-management tool is available. For example, an 8-year-old stepchild once shared, "I feel lonely for my Mom when I visit Dad, but if I keep busy and playing, the feelings go away." This was a wise youngster.

The journey from infancy to young adulthood is very much about learning to manage feelings appropriately. Everyone should expect a baby to cry when hungry or uncomfortable, and everyone should expect a teenager to wait patiently for supper to be served (or even better, join in the preparation to speed up the process) without complaints or whines. A 2-year-old is easily forgiven (although not rewarded) for a tantrum, but such behavior is not appropriate for a 6-year-old.

Self-management is about control and expression, not about just one or the other. There has been some confusion in the last few decades about the value of "letting go" or "letting it all hang out." *Emotional regulation* means sharing authentic emotions in ways likely to get prosocial outcomes. The mere unfiltered expression of emotion is not routinely therapeutic and is rarely a sign of emotional intelligence.

Managing anger is a common family therapy goal. Most often, parents believe that a self-management strategy such as hitting a punching bag or allowing the child to yell will help the child diminish angry feelings. In fact, despite a widespread belief in catharsis, it is incorrect and illogical. Anger management has at least two goals. One is to get over it. The other is to use the angry energy in a productive way.

Consider a rather silly contrast. What if I want to get over being happy? Should I laugh and smile more? Obviously, engaging in the components of an emotion produces more of the same emotion. To counter or reduce a feeling, people must engage in thoughts and actions that compete with the undesired feeling. Yelling and hitting are likely to increase not decrease anger.

The first step in anger reduction and constructive redirection is to label the feeling and to understand its origin. Am I frustrated, disappointed in self or others, embarrassed, or ashamed? All these emotions can "feel like" anger. Do I imagine someone else is responsible for these feelings or can I recognize myself as the source? Whatever the source, the solution is personal. Deep breathing, thinking aloud of positive and peaceful thoughts, a focus on desired end states, time outs, and a realistic appraisal of personal goals are all appropriate strategies to recommend to a family dealing with anger issues.

Parents can be urged to overtly model how they talk to themselves in times of stress. They do this to help the child learn effective self-management tools.

PARENT: I'm feeling frustrated by this problem. Hmm . . . I think I'll have to concentrate harder and work at it some more. Wow, it feels good to accomplish this! It took a lot of work and concentration, but I got it done!

PARENT: Oh no! I broke my glass . . .. I will take three deep breaths and count to 10. Then I'll be calm and clean it up.

SOCIAL AWARENESS

Social awareness entails understanding situational dynamics and other peoples' worldviews and feeling states. Understanding situational dynamics means the person can scan an interpersonal context and figure out what is happening. Is this a somber event or a celebration? Are people involved in tense exchanges or are they being silly and teasing toward one another? Is this a setting that calls for rather reserved and proper behavior or are people expected to be casual and boisterous? Most people learn this level of social awareness by practicing good listening skills—that is, they engage their brains before they engage their mouths.

Children need instruction about what to expect in varying settings. It is no favor to allow children to wander around a fine restaurant in the same way they may be allowed to wander around the playground of a fast-food restaurant. Social awareness is honed though practice and high expectations.

Empathy is the other key skill and virtue associated with social awareness. *Empathy* means having a deep connection to others' experiences, feelings, and perspectives. It is a strength that provides family members with many advantages—most importantly, the ability to be compassionate. Compassion is a vital antidote to chronic anger and polarizing conflicts. Without compassion, a family member's focus is on justifying his or her own position rather than on understanding different perspectives. Empathy can help family members become more flexible in problem solving by allowing them to develop sympathetic insights into each other's situations.

A technique that facilitates empathy during and between sessions is role-reversal enactment. The family is instructed as follows:

THERAPIST: The next time this fight starts, I want you to stop talking. You will know you're angry because you'll be breathing faster and probably feeling hot. Your voice might be louder or it might be shaking. Those are signals to notice. As soon as you realize what's happening, change roles. You parent, be the child. You child, be the parent. Each of you must stay in the new role and say what you want to happen that will make you happy.

Many families need some in-session enactments of this to perfect the switch, but most are eventually able to adopt it as an empathy-increasing strategy at home. It has the additional benefit of making family members laugh as they recognize some of the humor in their past dance of anger. Because positive emotions allow for more creative problem solving, non-derogatory humor is a good thing.

Children with high empathy skills are not hostile or aggressive toward others (Goldstein, 1999). Parents must be purposeful in developing empathy skills in children, especially in children with difficult temperaments. Children who are feeling- and other-oriented find empathy easier than children who are more cognitive- or self-oriented. Beginning with what the child does well and expanding upon the strength makes building empathy easier. For cognitively oriented children, making use of current events provides a platform for developing empathy. Parents can pick an issue in the news for a family or one-on-one discussion. The family discusses the plight of people made homeless by floods or who are hungry because of drought.

Parents can ask specific questions to help their children understand that others are confronted with very difficult situations. "How would we manage if we didn't have a house? What happens when there is no electricity? What would we feel if our house was flooded?" The point is not to frighten children, but to bring them closer to an experience that others are confronting. We recall being told to finish our food because "children are starving in China." This statement, despite its rather odd model of causality (i.e., If I eat, are they less hungry?), was obviously an attempt by our parents to put us in touch with the difficult situation faced by children our ages, but a half a world away. Our Depression-generation parents also reflected the deprivations and anxieties of that time to us as a way to increase our gratitude for current plenty and, we imagine, our sympathy for those in need.

Although empathy training is important at all ages and for all children, therapists should caution parents not to dwell on situations that heighten a child's existing anxieties, like losing their parents. Anxious children and those with attachment issues will not develop empathy from such discussions; they will merely suffer greater anxiety about their own situation.

One such youngster we treated in family therapy had been allowed to watch the video of the 9/11 tragedy over and over with accompanying discussions of all the lost parents and orphaned children resulting from the attack. His reaction was anger and serious acting-out behavior, not empathy for the orphaned children. The issue of his own elusive and unpredictable parent was much too close to his young concerns to allow room for others.

Parents of such children can discuss other matters, however, with good result. For example, families could discuss what it would be like for their family to go to a new country where they were not welcomed but had to stay in order to make enough money to live. They can also discuss what it feels like to be a new child at school or the newest member of a sports team. The point of these discussions is for children (and some adults) to develop from egocentrism to a position of being other-centered.

SOCIAL SKILLS

This final component of emotional intelligence represents a vast area of research and practice that has psychological roots in Bandura's (1973) work in social learning theory. There are many discrete social skills ranging from beginning social skill levels that include listening, saying thank you, and asking a question through advanced skills that include asking for help and convincing others. There are skills for dealing with feelings such as expressing affection and dealing with fear and skill alternatives to aggression that include asking permission and keeping out of fights. There are also skills for dealing with stress such as standing up for a friend or dealing with an accusation and advanced planning skills including setting a goal or making a decision.

This brief sampling of skills comes from a particularly effective and practical approach of teaching social skills developed by Goldstein and his colleagues (e.g., Goldstein, 1999; McGinnis & Goldstein, 1990). In addition to providing an exhaustive list of skills that must be learned for successful living, Goldstein combines a skill-learning approach with empathy training and character or moral development education.

Learning social skills depends on having good models, having opportunities to rehearse, and receiving corrective reinforcement. Family interactions can provide all these conditions if family members have the right information. Goldstein's approach can be taught to families and practiced within and between sessions.

Arnold Goldstein's (1999) social-skill contributions furthered our field by showing that the enactment of skills, while important, was not sufficient to predict generalization of the skills to multiple settings. Poor skills had to be replaced, new skills had to be learned, and new understandings reflecting increased levels of empathy and a sense of responsibility toward others had to be internalized for success. More recent applications of Goldstein's *Aggression Replacement Training* (Goldstein & Glick, 1987; Goldstein, Nensén, Daleflod, & Kalt, 2004; Reddy & Goldstein, 2001) have proved promising with families (Calame & Parker, 2003). The key message for families and therapists is that social skills must be taught in behavioral, emotional, and cognitive areas and must be grounded in a moral decision-making framework that highlights the importance of empathy.

PARENTAL SUPPORT AND GUIDANCE

Research on parental involvement identifies two key dimensions of support and guidance[3] that consistently predict children's and adolescents' well-being and optimal functioning. Supportive parents who employ the right kind of guidance increase their children's academic achievement (e.g., Bean, Bush, McKenry, & Wilson, 2003; Kim, Brody, & Murry, 2003) and self-esteem (e.g., Bean et al., 2003) and decrease depression (Mounts, 2004; Zimmerman, Ramirez-Valles, Zapert, & Maton, 2000).

Support embodies the parents' communication of warmth and acceptance toward their children. Support is identified as a powerful component of effective parenting in international studies and studies of U.S. ethnic groups (e.g., Garber, Robinson, & Valentiner, 1997; Gray & Steinberg, 1999; Herman, Dornbusch, Herron, & Herting, 1997). Parental communication of acceptance and caring is associated with children who are less depressed and display less externalizing problems regardless of ethnicity or socioeconomic status (Barber, Stolz, & Olsen, 2005; Bean et al., 2003; Kim & Cain, 2008; Kim et al., 2003; Mounts, 2004; Zimmerman et al., 2000; Gonzales, Deardorff, Formoso, Barr, & Barrera, 2006).

---

3. The research literature uses the term *control*, however we prefer the term *guidance*.

Guidance is often termed *control* in the literature. We prefer the term *guidance* because control implies a level of causality that is rarely accurate in parent-child relationships. Further, the idea of control suggests that increasing force will drive correct responses. This reasoning can lead to abusive interactions through first-order change beliefs as reviewed in Chapter 1. Control may be a reasonable construct in the physical science metaphor of therapy, but most skilled parents come to understand that control is an illusion. The most we can strive for, as our children grow, are to be extremely influential forces in their lives.

Based upon European American family samples, the concept of parental guidance has been subdivided into behavioral and psychological guidance (Barber et al., 2005; Schaefer, 1965). *Behavioral guidance* refers to parents structuring the child's world in ways that support the him/her acting appropriately by placing him/her in a context that supports good behavior (e.g., child-proofing rooms where toddlers live). Other examples of behavioral guidance are monitoring or supervising the child, knowing the child's whereabouts, or knowing what a child is doing at a particular location. These behavioral guidance techniques have been found to be universally helpful—for example, they have been associated with better child functioning across a number of settings (Barber, 1997; Garber et al., 1997; Steinberg, Dornbusch, & Brown, 1992; Steinberg, Mounts, Lamborn, & Dornbusch, 1991). Behavioral guidance is associated with helping children avoid problems with delinquency in African American (e.g., Eccles, Early, Frasier, Belansky, & McCarthy, 1997; Mason, Cauce, Gonzales, & Hiraga, 1996) and European American families (Barber, Stolz, Olsen, & Maughan, 2004; Weiss & Schwartz, 1996).

Psychological guidance, on the other hand, refers to structuring the internal experiences of the child. The descriptions of psychological guidance take on a rather negative tone as intrusions into the child's internal processes. The items used for measuring this construct have some resemblance to Minuchin's (1974) concept of *enmeshment*.[4] Therapists must use developmental and culturally competent judgment in this area, however. Enmeshment or some "mind reading" is necessary with very young children whose very existence depends on the parents' accurate assessment of their internal states. It also seems to be true that different cultures find varying levels of enmeshment expected and helpful.

High levels of psychological guidance have been found to be negative for European American children and adolescents (Barber et al., 2005) but not

---

4. Minuchin describes *enmeshment* as people's unhelpful blending of identities represented by nonindependent experiences of emotions or thoughts.

for African American adolescents (Bean, Barber, & Crane, 2006). Although this research is more suggestive than conclusive, it may be that collective[5] cultural groups find that parental involvement in the thoughts and feelings of children, even into their late teens (and perhaps beyond), is part of being a strong family. The high level of psychological guidance in a family probably requires closeness of the family through more of the lifetime of the child for the guidance to be functional.

The "right" amount and type of guidance seems to vary depending on the family's cultural heritage and level of acculturation. Some type of behavioral guidance is critical from the minimum of knowing where a child is, who she/he is with, and what she/he is doing, to psychological guidance in helping an adolescent know the correct manner of feeling. Family therapists must be attuned to the family's cultural expectations about both forms of guidance. Promoting increased behavioral monitoring seems always safe while supporting parents' efforts to structure their children's feeling states may or may not be useful.

MAXIMIZING MODELING

In several of the previously described between-session assignments, parents were asked to be positive models for their children. In fact, this is one of the greatest gifts a parent can give a child—a powerful template or blueprint that guides or at least gives options for the child's future.

Being a good model does not mean being perfect. In fact, a *coping model* is more effective than a perfect model (Meichenbaum, 1971). A *coping model* means that the model makes dilemmas, confusions, and mistakes overt to the observer so the observer understands that the path to a goal is not effortless and smooth. The observer learns that success depends on persistence and on developing alternative paths to desired states.

A parent who can think out loud about the process of moving from confused, frustrated, or slightly anxious through comforting, supportive self-statements and ending with self-congratulatory words with a pleased affect is a great coping model (Kazdin, 1973; Sarason, 1973). In contrast, a *perfect* or *mastery model* communicates that effective people do not need to expend effort or develop coping strategies. Children are best served by learning that confident self-encouragement and effort are part of any complex task.

---

5. Collective cultures focus more on the self in relation to the group (e.g., Asian American, Latino/a American, African American).

Parents who can share the process of recovering from a mistake provide invaluable modeling especially for anxious children. When parents model how to deal with spilled milk, a broken glass, or a lost object it gives children direction about how to promote their self-efficacy and -worth. An only child or first child does not have the older sibling to observe making clumsy errors and, therefore, must learn from a parent that to err and recover is the human condition.

Decision making provides another modeling event for parents to exhibit between sessions. Understanding how the family makes decisions and how families of origin made decisions can help clarify the strengths in their process and what they may wish to change. The goal of an improved decision-making process is to find ways of including all family members in important discussions.

Obviously, certain decisions are delegated to parents or the executive subsystem—families are not ideally democracies. Further, because of certain families' cultures, older people may have privilege in decision making or males or females may have more influence. A person with special physical or psychological needs may be the linchpin of decision making. Lessons from the extended families may provide a playbook of sorts that says father knows best about the external world and mother manages the home-front decisions. Many models of decision making appear to work in families, but most bear some investigation. Every culture, family, and person can evolve to a higher level of thriving. Reflective discussions that include the appropriate family members can be productive change events.

Feminist therapy approaches advocate asking family members to be aware of the consequences of the privilege given to family members based upon societal or cultural expectations. As family therapists, we must be constantly aware of the power and privileges that our dominant culture normalizes for certain members and lifestyles. Hare-Mustin (1994) notes that our "society privileges a discourse of heterosexual relations, obscures a discourse of female desire, and promotes a discourse of female victim-ization" (p. 24). The unexamined expectations held by family members and therapists can confine, stifle, and even harm individuals in a family. A therapist who is merely curious about the privileges of certain family members can open up the examination process. The role-reversal assign-ment described earlier in the chapter can be modified to start between-session conversations about decision making in a family and allow for parental modeling.

The decision-making process contains at least two invaluable steps: thinking ahead to consequences of the action and thinking about how the decision affects others. The process of decision making is often a balancing of individual pros and cons. Family cohesion and decision-making skills increase by revealing the decision-making process. Children can learn the importance of thinking about others and self while considering the consequences of a decision. This provides modeling for empathy and the importance of self-interest. A therapist can assign some decision-making tasks between parents and children.

THERAPIST: Here's what I want you all to try this week. You guys are wondering how to decide on how many times you can afford to eat out. The kids would like to eat out a lot and the grownups seem to prefer eating at home. I want the grownups to talk with the kids about how they make this decision. Then I want the children to do the same. Both of you have to consider the consequence of both decisions—money, nutrition, time, good food, taste, and so on. Come and tell me about what you learn about each other next week. Don't reach a final decision until we talk about it.

This type of between-session enactment can be very enjoyable. It demands that a parent and child take turns considering the consequences of various decisions out loud. The sharing clearly communicates parental values and the listening communicates respect.

Although a skill associated with emotional intelligence is thinking before talking—that is, don't say everything that pops into consciousness—parenting is a time of revealing thoughts and reevaluating their worth as guides for family development. A coping model can state something aloud and then correct the statement to make it more self-supportive or caring toward others.

MOTHER: I lost patience with Grandma this morning and cut off our conversation. I think I will call her back right now because I know she really likes our phone calls to her.

Concern for others can be modeled in many ways. When a fire truck or ambulance siren is heard, saying, "I hope it is a false alarm" communicates a thoughtfulness to children that is likely to be remembered for life.

CATCHING YOUR CHILD BEING GOOD

An important technique that has helpful benefits for families is the pattern of *catching children being good*. The technique benefits the family members by focusing their attentional processes toward finding and actively supporting positive behaviors (and *exceptions* to their presenting problem). Attending to positive behaviors means that family members enhance their relationship with each other by increasing their positive interactions. Catching children being good demands the child be noticed and praised for performing or approximating positive behaviors. It also demands that, to the extent possible, low-level negative behaviors are ignored.

This assignment is disarmingly simple, but it is actually rather difficult to enact. Parents get into patterns of noticing and responding to their children's disruption and actually avoid interacting with them when they are well-behaved. Exerting the energy to change this pattern is taxing. Further, it takes courage to believe that positive behaviors can replace the negative behaviors quickly enough to preserve family integrity.

The best praise is specific. For example, "I really love the way you are using your words to solve this problem." Further, the most effective praise links the behavior to a family value: "When you use your words to solve a problem, I can see that you are a kind and thoughtful person." This verbal formula links the child's behavior with the family virtue.

The technique of catching them being good can also be taught to the children as *catch your parent being good*. Parents must overtly commit to making some improvements—for example, increasing patience or time with the children. Children are instructed to praise examples of their parents' success very lavishly but to ignore failures. If parents seem to be hesitant about children praising them for positive behaviors, remind them that this process helps the children think about good behaviors and appreciate their parents more.

CONFLICT MANAGEMENT

All human interactions contain some conflict. Although conflict can be experienced as painful, identification and resolution of conflict are often the family's best opportunity for growth. Conflict must, however, be managed so that it does not deteriorate into aggression, withdrawal, or a verbal pattern of humiliation (Gottman, 1994; Gottman & Levenson, 1999). Ideally, conflicts are resolved so that both parties feel like winners.

The goal in therapy is to help the family practice a process of conflict management and resolution that gets many alternative opinions into the discussion with each opinion being greeted with curiosity and respect. An additional goal is for family members to hear disagreements without experiencing criticism or disloyalty. Gottman and Levenson's (1999) work suggests that highly functioning families are able to keep making positive statements to each other (five positive to every negative statement) even during conflictual periods. On the other hand, families with a trajectory toward divorce express less than one positive statement to every negative statement during conflictual times.

Therapists must remember that families differ in their tolerance for conflict and heated discussion. Certain cultural groups seem to promote their children's energetic and even aggressive disputes as evidence of intelligence. Highly energized conflicts must include or be countered by experiences of validation. For example, what does it mean in the family to "lose" an argument? Is that person diminished in some way? How is that experience countered? Other families' act as if uncovering a disagreement will risk extreme upset and polarization. Some follow a rule of focusing only on the positive because, once uttered, negative statements cannot be rescinded. Conflict-avoidant families need tools and support for knowing how to approach differences openly. The variety of skills and meanings that families have and attach to conflict make it a fruitful subject for therapeutic discussion. Whatever the family model, it is clear that all family members need conflict management and resolution skills inside and outside of the family.

Teaching and then asking family members to practice the classic "I statement" communication skill is a useful basic step. The family member who wants a change in some family pattern must take the risk of raising it for family discussion, but he or she should do so by identifying the issue as a personal one and include in the statement his or her desired solution (e.g., "I am feeling very anxious because you seem to be spending so much time away from the family. I really want us to be close by spending one evening on the weekend together."). An important rule for conflict resolution is to use deep breathing to stay relaxed and speak in a quiet, solemn tone. Negative affect tends to overshadow content, making defensiveness more likely than curiosity. Families may need time-outs when discussing conflictual topics. Asking for a brief respite from a heated discussion is a good strategy. Withdrawing from or stonewalling certain topics is, however, not helpful to positive family life. If a time-out is requested, then the person requesting the time-out needs to be responsible for reinitiating the discussion within a stated short period of time.

After several in-session practice sessions, an out-of-session conversation started like this:

COLLEGE SOPHOMORE DAUGHTER: I want to live in the dorms at my college. I want to experience more independence and practice my skills at living on my own.

FATHER: This is not the right time to talk about this. You know how I feel about your leaving the house and you can also see that I am very busy now.

DAUGHTER: I know you have strong feelings and I know they come from loving me. I am feeling the need to be more grown up, but I can put off the conversation for a few hours so we can have a relaxed and unhurried discussion.

FATHER: I appreciate hearing that you know I love you. What does being more grown up mean to you?

DAUGHTER: And I love you very much. Being grown up means washing my own clothes, determining my own curfews, choosing my own friends, spending as much time as I want on the computer or in the library, and generally being my own person.

FATHER: You can do all of this now, as far as I can tell. What about making your own money? That's the stumbling block I see.

DAUGHTER: You are right in a lot of ways. And I do have a financial plan that includes my getting a job, taking out a student loan, and asking you to continue paying tuition.

FATHER: I'm impressed that you have thought of all of that. I guess your Mother and I feel a little abandoned or rejected when you talk about moving out.

DAUGHTER: That's the last thing I want to do. What I want is for all of us to feel good about this new adventure. I know I'll need your advice on a million things while I do this and actually need your advice for a very long time.

FATHER: Okay, let me talk to your Mother. She will not like this and will probably be crying about it for a year—it's hard to see you grow up and leave us.

This excerpt illustrates a good exchange. The daughter and the father show skills in listening to each other, communicating empathy, restating each other's positions, and revealing their concerns and solutions. It is noteworthy that the daughter in this family moved from an earlier position of entitlement and privilege (i.e., her family owed her a college education of her design) to the one illustrated in the excerpt. She seemed to grow over the course of therapy in both empathy for her parents' financial situation and in her skills in presenting a problem.

What if a win-win solution is not evident? Systems of decision making when both parties cannot win can be in a simple taking-turns format (e.g.,

"Last week you picked pizza so this week I'm picking Chinese.") or deciding that, until coming to an agreement, a decision cannot occur (e.g., "We'll just keep looking for a couch that we both like," assuming both want a couch).

If taking turns seems the only reasonable course for the family then there are some caveats to consider. The first is that a written history needs to be part of the decision so that the next decision will not include an argument about whose turn it is. The second caveat is that all decisions are not of the same importance. The parties need to rate the importance of the issue on a scale from 1 to 5 so that there is some parity from decision to decision. Families can help set anchor points for what a 1 or a 5 means. Choosing take-out food may be a 1 on the scale, but setting curfews may be a 5.

Waiting for unanimity may also require a postscript. Some conflicts can be put on hold, others cannot. For example, although a family can use the existing couch, it can't sustain patterns of verbal or physical aggression until everyone comes to the same conclusions. A familiar family battle-ground concerns children's completion of chores. The fights are overtly about taking out the garbage, but they are really about autonomy and responsibility. Parents and children often couch their statements like this:

PARENT: You never do what you are supposed to do. You say you want privileges but you don't show any responsibility.

CHILD: I can't do anything that pleases you. It's never enough. You never let me do what I want.

This is an example of an exchange unlikely to lead to a win-win resolution. The parent must set some standards for behavior and have high expectations about the child completing assigned tasks. The child predictably chafes at any restrictions or conditions attached to growing autonomy. We often tell families embroiled in such dilemmas that they are doing exactly the right thing—both of them. The parent is promoting responsibility and the child is seeking autonomy. The world of family development is as it should be.

The way for this family to move to better conflict resolution is to switch the focus of their conversations. The child knowing that the parent wants to hear about behaviors couched in terms of responsibility and the parents knowing that the child wants confirmation that his ability to be autonomous is recognized.

CHILD: Today I forgot to take out the garbage. Sorry, Dad. I did remember something important, though. I called Grandma on her birthday." (Responsible in acknowledging problem and success.)

PARENT: Take it out now. Nice job calling Grandma. You did that even though I forgot to remind you." (Keeping standards and acknowledging autonomy.)

Some families decide which course of action to follow by intensity—that is, the person who feels the strongest about the issue gets to decide. This works for families with fairly similar temperaments. If, however, one person regularly feels more strongly about everything, then the intensity rule can eventually leave the less intense party resentful. If intensity is the deciding factor, its use must be monitored closely.

Influence through intensity can manifest itself in very destructive ways. Threatening behaviors and actual physical violence are chillingly effective in gaining control of family conflict resolution and decision making. While the earlier injunction related to therapist sensitivity to varying family norms bears repeating, therapists must be clear with clients that if they see physical violence within a session or learn about violence between sessions, they are bound by state laws to report it to the appropriate authorities. Occasionally, families have been referred to us because of a history of violence. The same strategies outlined throughout this volume are useful with such families. A difference is that the therapist must be absolutely clear that violence will not be tolerated as an influence strategy or as a response to stress. This message should be assertive but can be positive.

THERAPIST: You are here for a lot of reasons. One is that the court has ordered it. But I can tell that you want a good family and a happy family. All other families have struggles. A special thing about your family is that you have used a very destructive way of trying to make things work in your family. The good news is that you've learned that using violence and keeping secrets is not an option. The bad news is that using threats and violence is a habit that you'll have to break right away. I will not be able to keep any secrets from the authorities. Thousands of families just like you have learned to be happy and successful. You can, too, even though it will be hard. There are ways you already know and new ways that you will learn that will make this happen.

BETWEEN SESSION WORK FOR THERAPISTS: ALLIANCE WITH SCHOOLS

All therapy approaches may require planning and coordination of services for clients between their therapy visits. This coordination may be with medical doctors, social service agencies, probation services, and so on.

Family therapy practice may elicit more urgency for connections with other professionals as the needs of the family and its individual members are analyzed. A very frequent between-session demand for family therapists is to consult with school personnel. Many families actually approach therapy only at the direct or indirect suggestion of teachers or school counselors. Many of the problems that concern parents occur at school as well as at home.

The most powerful approaches to alleviating children's mental health and behavioral success encourage strong alliances among families, mental health personnel, and schools (Barnard, 2004; Hill, Castellino, Lansford, Nowlin, Dodge, Bates, et al., 2004; U.S. Public Health Service, 2000). Thus far, the information shared in this volume illustrates building the family-mental health service alliance. Involving educators in this partnership can be a potent addition (Carlson & Christenson, 2005; Christenson, 2003).

Therapists have several avenues to explore in building this partnership. One avenue consists of instructing parents in the skills and importance of closely working with school personnel to improve their children's academic and social situations. Such work involves attending parent teacher and special education placement and planning meetings, cooperating with home–school communication programs (e.g., signing off on homework, implementing home-based reinforcement for school success), and generally staying informed and involved in their child's academic progress. The best outcomes arise from relationships in which parents feel empowered by their understanding of what schools expect from their children and how they might be involved (National Institute of Mental Health, 2001).

Although many middle and upper class, majority culture parents often have easy access to participating in all of the above, obstacles for poor, immigrant, or otherwise marginalized parents can be daunting. The difficulties may grow from a family's perceptions or confusion about school policies or the school's commitment to their children or can come from a school that has not developed a welcoming structure to support parent involvement. Parents, especially of troubled adolescents often report being exhausted by constant, negative contacts from a school. They choose to withdraw, perhaps, feeling that their energies are better spent on the home front. School personnel, likewise, develop low expectations about parent involvement and sometimes fail to use creative or energetic strategies to promote family connections to school-based programs.

The ways schools work are not obvious to recent immigrants or those with limited English language skills. Immigrant families may, for any number of understandable reasons, imagine that their only role is to deliver their children to the door of the school and expect that professionals will do the rest. Therapists can play an important role in explaining school policies and expectations to such parents.

Whatever the obstacles, however, compelling evidence suggests that children's needs are best met when families are empowered to connect with schools (Hoagwood, 2005; Jenson & Hoagwood, 2008; Jeynes, 2005). How can a positive family therapist assist?

First, the therapist can be the convener of conjoint behavioral consultation efforts within a school (Sheridan & Kratochwill, 2008). This well described approach brings children's caretakers and teachers into an organized conversation that results in children's strengths at home and at school being identified and developed by both parents and teachers. The approach is consistent with positive family therapy and has received consistent empirical support as an effective school-based practice (Garbacz, Woods, Swanger-Gagne, Taylor, Black, & Sheridan; in press. Sheridan & Burt, in press; Sheridan, Clarke, Burt, 2008; Sugai, Horner, Dunlap, Hieneman, Lewis, Nelson, et al.; 2000). Essentially, parents and teachers meet at least four times together. They jointly identify a child's strengths that, when enhanced, will leverage success at home and at school. They build a coordinated plan with a strong home-school communication strategy, implement it, and evaluate its effectiveness. The family therapist can play a valuable role by keeping the process moving and ensuring the implementation of the evaluation strategies (e.g., Schoenwald, Henggeler, Brondino, & Rowland, 2000).

Another role the therapist can play is as a consultant to the client child's teacher. Obviously, the therapist, family, and the school must coordinate permissions so that privacy is protected. Further, a therapist who has limited experience in schools might seek collaboration from a school psychologist or social worker to promote successful connections with teachers, principals, special education teachers, or other specialists (Evans, Sapia, Axelrod, & Glomb, 2002; Zins, Weissberg, Wang, & Walberg, 2004).

If a face-to-face or phone meeting can be scheduled with the child's classroom teacher, the therapist may gather additional data useful for family therapy intervention planning and share information with the teacher about handling the challenges the client is presenting in the classroom. Many comprehensive resources are available for therapists to hone their school consultation skills (e.g., Erchul & Sheridan, 2008; Weare, 2000). A few general guidelines are useful to consider, however, when planning a school consult.

Educators are often quite sensitive to externalizing problems that children exhibit. Being a lone adult with 20–35 children creates a press that causes acting out children to get attention (Pullis, 1992). A quick resolution of negative, disruptive behavior is often a teacher's first goal. The school-based strategies that have the best supportive evidence in assisting these children to develop better academic and social outcomes are tangible rewards, praise, monitoring behavior, time-out, giving effective commands, psycho-education, and response cost (Kratochwill, Albers, & Shernoff, 2004; Weisz, 2004).

Teachers may need some assistance to apply these powerful strategies in their classes. The consultation skill, like the therapy skill, is figuring out which of these has the highest acceptability to the teacher and is the best match to the current classroom situation and teacher skills. A few words of elaboration about each practice may be useful.

Tangible rewards are common in many classrooms. They are often delivered based on individual or group behavior. Sometimes, the individual is randomly picked and is the one who earns (or does not earn) rewards (stickers, time at a favorite activity, popcorn, etc.) for the entire class. Whole class programs of tangible rewards are quite powerful. If, however, the client child has social relation problems, it is usually best not to have other children's rewards depend on the client's behavior – at least not initially. This just invites an escalation of negative interactions should the client fail to reach the threshold for the class-wide rewards.

Praise should be specific and tied to an agreed upon outcome. "Thank you for raising your hand, Todd. I really appreciate your patience," is a better praise statement than, "You are great." We know from research on relationships that persist versus those that end in divorce that positive statements outnumber negative statements by 5:1. Although analogous research has not been done in classrooms, the ratio is a good aspirational goal to share with teachers.

Monitoring behavior means noticing what children are doing—especially catching children being good. Good monitoring also includes catching the beginning stages of a negative behavior, "stopping it low to prevent it high" (Goldstein, 1999). The best teachers have a withitness quality that allows them to teach a small group, but still pay attention to individuals in other groups. The difficulty of monitoring can leave even successful behavior change programs abandoned by teachers. A solution to extra workload can be teaching a child to self-monitor. The child can be taught to note examples of good behavior, thus, relieving the teacher of some of the vigilance.

Time-out is a time honored educational technique that means excluding a child from the positive interaction of the classroom for a brief period to allow the child to regain composure and miss the excitement of engagement. Time out works only if the classroom is "time-in." That is, the class activities must be motivating enough that the child hates to miss them. A time-out chair is often placed near the teacher's desk, or sometimes the child is excluded entirely by being sent to an in-school suspension area or the child has recess time reduced. The exclusion time should be brief.

A consulting therapist can ask a teacher to role-play giving directions to a child. Even veteran teachers sometimes forget to give simple (one or two step) commands in a clear, pleasant, but unquestioning tone. A command has added weight if it follows the following formula.

"Ron, it is time for you to stop your math and go to the reading center. You have one minute to begin at the center. Thank you!"

"Ron, this is your second reminder. You must go to the reading center now and begin working or you will lose time at recess."

Many teachers err by phrasing commands as if they were questions, for example, "Are you ready to go to the reading center, Ron?" This is a weak command. Good commands are friendly, delivered in even tones, and accompanied by unwavering eye contact.

Psycho-education has many applications, but in the school context most often comprises social skills, character and moral education if the target child has disruptive behavior (see Goldstein, 1999). Parents can be the recipients of psycho-educational materials to help them gain greater appreciation of their child's challenges and promote their partnership in helping children practice new skills at home. Substantial information is also available about anxiety disorders, developmental disorders (e.g., autism, mental retardation), and attention disorders.

Finally, response cost is a behavioral strategy that essentially means that a child who engages in bad behavior loses rewards. For example, target children may start the day with 20 minutes of recess, but lose minutes if they fail to raise their hands or if they are disruptively disengaged from their work. Response cost can be implemented to a whole class using a variety of approaches. A popular example is a lottery system. To implement one period each day identified as the behavior game lottery times. Students each receive five strips of paper—a different color for each child. The strips represent good behavior points. The strips are placed on each child's desk. During the lesson, the teacher removes a strip for each behavioral infraction. Remaining strips are deposited in a jar or bowl. Every day or every week the teacher draws out a strip with the winner gaining some highly desirable prize (see Witt & Elliott, 1982 for details). Although we generally prefer noticing positives rather than negatives, response cost is effective because it provides a signal to children that they are not meeting their goals and it results in a positive consequence when they do meet goals.

Many book, article, and web resources exist that describe effective school based practices with externalizing and internalizing children (Adelman &

Taylor, 2000; Kratchowill, 2007; Rosenfield & Berninger, 2009; Rones & Hoagwood, 2000). School consultants are most effective when they know about evidence based practices, use the teachers' strengths, map their suggestions on to the teachers' needs, and provide follow up support as well as evaluation.

The interventions included in this chapter provide a rich collection of approaches to support family growth. The fundamental platform for family growth is family members' supportive involvement, use of supportive resources, behavioral guidance, knowledge about one another and ways to disagree. The methods presented in Chapter 3 provide options for helping families further their abilities and resources. The ideas preserve the integrity of the family through supportive environments while promoting the family cultural values through reflective discussions and openness to growth.

Positive Family Therapy
Case Examples

GOAL OF CHAPTER 4

Two cases are described in some detail, demonstrating the application of the techniques outlined in the previous chapters.

Key Concepts in Chapter 4: acculturation, cultural competence, *formalismo*, subgoals, meta-goals, miracle question, scaling questions, circular questions, agreeing with the client, systemic visualizations, presuppositional language, exception finding, catching the child being good.

INTRODUCTION

Chapter 4 presents parts of two cases. Both case studies are derived from family therapy research projects at a university clinic. The details and names are altered to protect the participants' identities. The first case represents a very common presentation for families in therapy. The second case is shared to illustrate some of the techniques used when there is a mismatch of culture and heritage language between the clients and therapists.

CASE ONE: TODD IS NUMBER ONE

The family initially called the university clinic concerned about their son's oppositional behavior. They described it as disrupting their home life. Pretherapy assessment in the clinic intake forms revealed the son of the heterosexual couple had a current diagnosis of Attention-Deficit Disorder

(ADD) and his behaviors were consistent with a diagnosis of Oppositional Defiant Disorder.

This family represents the most frequent referral issue that brings families into a therapy context—problematic externalizing child behaviors. These behaviors typically fit within the diagnosis of Oppositional Defiant Disorder and are often extreme enough to be considered conduct disordered. Often a comorbid diagnosis of ADD is present.

The presenting problems frequently include the parents and school personnel describing their trouble with the child's noncompliance and aggressive behavior. The parents arrive at our therapeutic door expressing feelings of anger directed at the child, each other, and the school personnel. The negative interactions reverberate continuously throughout the family system. The feelings of frustration at being unsuccessful parents fuel feelings of shame and doubt. Parents may remember what worked for them as children or they know what worked for their other child. The tried-and-true, common sense, never-failed-before approaches no longer work. The frustration becomes anger. Anger prompts flight-or-fight options—run away or at least deny the existence of a problem or engage in endless battles with the child and with the other parent. None of these choices create good parenting ideas. The child often feels the frustration of failing to gain positive attention and expresses the anxiety or anger through externalizing behaviors. Negative notoriety is better than no fame at all.

The following example is based upon a successful brief Positive Family Therapy treatment of a boy, Todd, and his biological mother and stepfather, referred to as dad. Todd's mother called for an appointment, stating that Todd was a 9-year-old European American boy who was having problems with his anger at school. When the family arrived for the first session, the parents listed Todd's many problems in their initial paperwork. Todd took medicine associated with his ADD diagnosis; he was argumentative, disobedient, and had frequent angry outbursts both at home and at school. Several times the parents were asked to remove Todd from school because he was deemed out of control. Socially, Todd was a loner. He played alone at recess and ate alone in the cafeteria.

The family moved into town upon the marriage of the parents 5 years ago. No extended family was nearby. The family culture was to be socially alone. No family contacts or friends ever visited their home. There were no friends that Todd played with at home. The parents had acquaintances at work but did not socialize with them after hours.

Todd collected and organized treasures/garbage that he would not throw away (e.g., used staples, electronic parts, rocks). The family finally sought help for Todd because of the insistence of better behavior from the school and his harming the pet cat. Todd's family met for five therapy sessions over a 7-week period. The family set goals each session and consistently reported meeting the goals either partially or fully. Although they were a multiproblem family, they became ideal clients.

The first session began with socializing and joining activities. Because the family was of European American ancestry and appeared fully acculturated to the majority culture, we made the assumption that the informality of first names and shaking of hands was appropriate from the initial meeting. These initial assumptions proved to be accurate. The family seemed relieved that we began slowly and positively without an anger outburst from Todd.

Conveying a hopeful attitude, I asked the father, mother, and Todd what they enjoyed doing and about their jobs. They described their interests and hobbies. I responded with sincere interest and follow-up questions to gain some details. Each person enjoyed my attention but only the mother seemed to listen attentively when others talked. Dad and Todd enjoyed talking about themselves but did not appear to listen to the others.

Todd especially liked the attention and interest I showed in his life. I thought that was a very good sign. Clearly positive social attention was important to him although his self-description and his parents' description of him gave no clue to that strength. He stated that he enjoyed collecting electronic objects. His mother would take him to the secondhand stores where he could buy broken items to disassemble and categorize the parts. Todd did not reveal any positive connection to his father or teacher. He stated often that the children at school teased him and it made him very angry.

During the socializing and joining activity, I was careful to display neutrality by demonstrating interest in each person's strengths. Even when I spoke with one person I used circular questions to include other family members in responding to the family member who was disclosing interests and strengths, such as asking who shares the strength and if each was aware of the strength in the other. After establishing rapport and discovering some individual and family strengths, I asked what they would like to accomplish with me. Even though the question is phrased in such a manner to elicit their goals, the inevitable answer is to list the problems they perceive in others.

THERAPIST (Asking generally to the family members): What would you like to accomplish with me? What goals would you like to accomplish by coming here?

MOTHER:[1] Well, Todd is a very smart boy. He has an IQ of 117! But Todd spends half his school day in special education classes because of his angry outbursts in class. His teacher tells us he yells in class, is rude, disrespectful, and argumentative. We have been called by the principal to bring him home many times because they said he was out of control.

THERAPIST: That must concern you a great deal. You have a wonderful son, a smart boy who is not using his abilities well. Is there anything else you feel you need to tell me? (Notice that I briefly validate that I heard a concern but I do not delve into the details or feelings surrounding the problem. I ask about other concerns, inviting issues but not encouraging in-depth descriptions of problems.)

MOTHER: Well, at home he argues with us a lot.

DAD: He is not responsible. He argues with me whenever I tell him to do something. And he never admits doing anything wrong. He has hurt our cat. (During the airing of Todd's problems, Todd's murmuring objections become louder and his movement in his chair more pronounced.)

DAD: Todd has a real problem with collecting objects like rocks, paper clips, and electronic parts. He won't ever throw anything away. His room is a junkyard and it spills into the rest of the house!

MOM: But he loves and is very nice to his pet parrot. (Mom shows some skill and insight into knowing that it is time to de-escalate Todd's increasingly negative emotions before they become aggressive behaviors.)

THERAPIST: He is good with his parrot? That is important. (While saying this I smile at Todd. Being kind to his pet is a strength, so I accentuate it.)

THERAPIST (Talking to Todd): Did you know that your mom thinks you are really good with your parrot, Todd? (This is a circular question in that I took information given by mom and fed it back into the family through Todd. This circular question acts as both an information probe and an intervention. Information is sought about Todd's knowledge of his mom's positive belief about him. The circular question acts as an intervention to clearly communicate a positive belief about Todd.)

TODD: My parrot likes me best! He likes mom next and he doesn't like dad much! (Todd likes the topic of his parrot and tells me more about him. However, dad would like to get back to business, the problems.)

---

1. Instead of using the first names of Todd's parents in the dialogue, we have used the generic mom and dad to simplify understanding while reading.

When strengths of Todd were mentioned, I smiled, became more attentive, and clearly revealed how impressed I was. When problems were stated I was solemn, moved very little, and asked very few questions. I allowed a few sentences about each problem topic then I asked, Is there anything else? I did not want to spend much time on the problems but I did not want to miss any signs of danger (e.g., suicide, homicide, abuse, trauma). Although it is imperative that the parents feel understood, the problems were not leading us to the help, which they expected of me.

I am not the only one who wishes to get through the problem description. His parents' listing of problems upsets Todd. He attempts to interrupt the statements of problems, especially when his dad lists them. Although Todd was choosing to be uninvolved initially, he joined in on the fault-finding or blame game when it was his turn.

TODD: Dad throws away my collections without asking me! I tell him no but he never listens. And he yells at me all the time. And my teacher never listens to me either. She never believes me. The kids always tease me and make fun of me. I hate them.

THERAPIST: Thanks for telling me what you are thinking, Todd. I can tell that you want people to be nicer to you at school and at home. It is very important to have people you enjoy being with. (turning to everyone) All of you have some things that you think could be different about the family—things that can make your life together better, more enjoyable, or fun for you.

Neither Todd nor his parents described any shortcomings of their own. This is not unusual. I did not ask any person to admit any shortcomings nor were there many follow-up questions asked about problems. Typically, I attempt to block hostile interactions that may occur. Fortunately, there were none in this session. I exhibited concern and respect to each person's perspective. I reassured them that family members inevitably see different concerns. They appeared comfortable that they had communicated their major worries. After about 20 to 25 minutes into the session I began to ask about goals specifically. I sense that they have each aired their primary concerns about each other. Now I begin to help them focus more squarely upon goals they would like to see in the family.

THERAPIST: What would you like to have happen today?
MOTHER: Well, I did not want much to happen because Todd was frightened about coming to therapy.

THERAPIST: That is a good idea. We don't want to go too fast. What were you hoping that in five years when you look back on coming in, you would say, I'm glad we did that! (Notice that I agree with the client. Agreement is great modeling for fostering cooperation.)

MOM: I would like for Todd to have higher self-esteem, behave better at school, reduce his anger and his frustration.

THERAPIST: So you would like Todd to be happier with himself, be success-ful in school, and be friendlier with his teacher and the other children. (Notice that I help state the goals in the positive, what mom would like for Todd to do. Reducing the occurrence of a behavior does not give a replacement behavior. When we get more specific I may ask mom to tell me explicitly what she wants. At this stage I am comfortable helping with the switch from negative goals to positive goals.)

MOM: Yes!

THERAPIST: How about you, dad? What goals do you have for your family today?

DAD: I would like for Todd to take responsibility for his actions. I want him to admit when he has done something wrong and clean up his mistakes.

THERAPIST: So you really like it when Todd is responsible and you think it is very important for him to develop that ability so that he can be a happier guy. (Notice that the restatement presupposes that Todd does act responsibly sometimes, maybe just once! Also, the addition of why dad would like Todd to be responsible is added. This addition of wanting Todd to be happier was missing when dad stated his goal and probably dad had never said or thought this overtly. However, he quickly endorses the linking of responsibility and happiness. Dad seems to be type cast in the family as more negative and punitive. Mom probably feels she needs to protect her sensitive son from her angry husband. The revelation of dad wanting his son to be happy begins the new social construction of dad. The way each member in the family is viewed predicts how each person's self-image will change. The suitable behavior that fits dad's new definition should follow.)

DAD: Yeah, that is right. I want him to be happier.

THERAPIST: You do!?! (turning to Todd) Did you know that your dad wants you to be happy Todd? (A circular question as an intervention.)

TODD: No.

THERAPIST: I'm so glad that your dad wants you to be happy! What would you like to have happen from coming here today, Todd?

TODD: I want the kids at school to quit teasing me. And I want the teachers not to yell at me anymore.

THERAPIST: So you'd like to have people at school be nicer to you and you'd like to be happier at school. What would you like to have better at home?

TODD Nothing.

THERAPIST (facing the parents): Did you know that Todd was happy with his home life? (Circular question as intervention)

PARENTS: No, that is a surprise!

THERAPIST (to Todd): That is wonderful, Todd. Did you see your parents smile? They really like it when you compliment or say something nice. I bet you didn't know that you could make them smile? (Circular question; Todd and parents laugh.)

Perhaps Todd was attempting to be noncooperative with the process by not suggesting any changes at home. However, we did not focus on the negative part of the communication. The communication was reframed into his liking home life. Later, Todd did volunteer again that dad was acting angrily toward him and he would like dad to be nicer, which I simplified into a happier home life. It was easier to inch back toward his involvement in the goal later. This section ends with the family laughing together over a positive behavior from Todd. This changed the affect in the room from tense to relief and mild happiness. Positive emotions were a good start for fostering creative thinking and possibly change.

The global issue of happiness is the first goal that was identified. In a contentious family, the first goal is often at a higher order of abstraction. Goals such as everyone feeling happier, acting kinder, and communicating better are initial *meta-goals*, which will have to be focused before progress is attained. However, celebrating having a meta-goal gives the family a feeling of movement and success midway through the first session! Additionally, a positive goal and a shared focus bring the family together. Mutual responsibility for a goal is much more acceptable than a problem focus. Focusing on reducing Todd's temper tantrums and oppositional behavior can easily create a negative focus that shames Todd. His accomplishments from a negative frame could create a feeling of resentment, not wanting to be the fall guy for the family. When focusing on a goal such as happiness the entire family can easily share the responsibility with pride. Everyone can enjoy taking credit for the change toward a family-wide positive goal.

After consolidating the meta-goal with Todd's family, I suggest that we begin with a small, specific goal at home because all three of them are at home and can work together on a goal. When asked about a goal that would make all three of them happier, the mother suggests that a nightly issue that inevitably ends in a tumultuous argument is getting Todd out of the shower. She would like exiting the shower resolved without conflict. The father agrees with the identified goal. Todd is hesitant. Todd knows that in the past he is the one who is asked to change when discussing the shower. So as the process unfolds I know that Todd will have to believe that he has something to gain in this process. Linking the shower back to Todd's desire to have a happier family will be the strategy. The subgoal of ending a shower peacefully will have to be solidly linked to the overall goal of family happiness, for each member of the family!

THERAPIST: So when you resolve the shower concern, how is this going to make everyone in family happier?

MOM: Well, I know that I'm going to be so happy when there is no yelling, threatening, and crying at shower time. That will make my evening much happier!

DAD: That is right. I won't have to be yelling and spending my whole evening trying to get you out of the shower!

THERAPIST: Wonderful! So you two will be happier. What will be happening that makes you happy? You told me what will *not* be happening. What will be going on that makes all three of you happier? Take away all the negative things. What will be happening that you like? (Moving a problem into a goal statement.)

MOM: That is difficult. I guess I will be happy because Todd will be happy.

THERAPIST: Okay, good. You will be happy when Todd is happy. I know you love for him to be happy. And when he is happy it makes you happy too! Did you know that Todd? Did you know that you can make your mom happy? She loves it when you are happy! (Circular question.)

TODD: No.

THERAPIST: Dad, what about you? What will be happening that makes you happy? All the negative parts are gone. What will be happening that makes you happy?

DAD: I don't know. I guess that I'll be happy because Todd is happy.

THERAPIST: Oh wonderful! You will be happy when Todd is happy, too. Wow! Todd you are really good at making your parents happy! (Presuppositional language.)

So this is great. Mom and dad are happy when Todd is happy. Now why is Todd happy?

(No Response)

THERAPIST: Okay, so we need to make sure Todd is happy. Now, Todd, when you were saying what you wanted when I first met you, you said that you did *not* want your dad to yell at you and act angry. I guess I forgot to ask you what you wanted him to do. How do you like him act?

TODD: I like it when dad plays video games with me.

THERAPIST: Great, you like to play games with your dad. Dad did you know that? Todd really likes it when you play video games? (Circular question.)

DAD: Yes.

THERAPIST: So Todd, what is it that you like about your dad when you guys play a game together? What is he doing that makes you happy?

TODD: *I* beat him in the games! (Everyone laughs.)

DAD: It's true. He is really good at those video games.

THERAPIST: Wow, you must be really good to beat your dad! Does your dad get mad at you when he loses?

TODD: Yeah! He gets really upset! (Todd laughs.)

DAD: No, I don't! You know that isn't true! (Mom agrees with dad.)

THERAPIST: Oh, Todd! So how does your dad act? Does he smile at you? Does he say nice things about you? About how good you are at the game? (Investigating a strength that involves the relationship of dad and Todd.)

TODD: Yeah, he does. He says I'm number one!

THERAPIST: And that makes you happy when he smiles at you and says you're number one?

TODD: Yeah . . .

THERAPIST: So that is what will make you happy at shower time, too! Is that right? Your dad smiling at you and saying you are number one? Maybe we could get your mom to do that, too! What do you think?

TODD: Yeah, she never says I'm number one!

THERAPIST: This is great, Todd! Dad did you know that you make Todd happy when you smile at him? He really likes that! Is that right, Todd? (Repetition of the positive influence each person has with the other is important to cement the understanding. When negative interactions have been the focus for a long period of time, the possibility of positive influence has been forgotten.)

This sequence demonstrates the negotiation of an initial subgoal. The important features are that all three family members thought that the shower interaction was negative and all believed that they would be happier with a calm, peaceful shower. Notice that the parents forgot initially that Todd needed to feel happier about the change. That is typical. Often parents forget that everyone needs to see the goal as helpful to invest in its success. Also, if everyone clearly benefits through more positive affect, the progress once made will be incorporated into the family's ongoing process. Fredrickson's (1998) broaden and build theory suggests the experiences built upon positive affect will even generalize to other activities in the family. *Escalation theory* describes small changes growing through mutual interactions to create larger changes.

Now there is a tentative commitment from everyone that exiting the shower cooperatively could be a worthy goal on the road to family happiness. As the session progressed, the details of the problematic behavior were examined and transformed into subgoals. The parents wanted Todd to leave the shower when asked and to pick up his objects from the shower. This behavior would be a wonderful sign of responsibility. Todd would presently take several hours in the shower if allowed to leave on his own accord. At times they would allow the hot water to run out so that he would leave peacefully. They would like for him to stay only 30 minutes. Also, Todd fills the shower with rocks and other objects from his collections. They would like for him to clean up his treasures from the family's only shower.

Todd was not willing to commit to the goal of leaving the shower clean and peacefully after 30 minutes. I mentally noted Todd's misgivings but did not verbally focus on his hesitation. Todd saw there was a problem about showering but the problem was his parents' inflexibility. He was not yet willing to endorse the goal that his parents and the therapist negotiated of a shorter shower time and cleaning the shower upon leaving.

The next step is to clearly lay out the process to achieving the goal of a happy shower time. The parents were asked when the last time Todd "took responsibility" (parents phrase) for getting out of the shower. This is the *finding of exceptions* (De Jong & Berg, 1998)—that is, when was this positive behavior last accomplished. Exceptions reveal the family's strengths in accomplishing goals.

There are many ways to accomplish goals. We hope to find a strength that accomplishes the goal and engenders positive feelings. Unfortunately, the parents could not remember one time that Todd got out of the shower peacefully. So finding a similar goal that the family had accomplished may reveal a helpful skill set. Getting out of the shower could be conceptualized as a time of transition. When asked about the process of transitioning from one activity to another like leaving an activity to commence eating dinner they said that there are times they accomplished this peacefully. I became very curious and excited about the times when Todd was "responsible." Mother stated that Todd was more responsible when dad was not at home. Todd agreed enthusiastically, reporting that he was always responsible when dad was not at home. Mother corrected him, saying Todd was sometimes more responsible when dad was not home. I focused on the report of responsibility rather than the disagreement about amount. I asked Todd what it was that his mother does that helped him behave responsibly. Todd answered that his mother did not tell him to throw things away. I did not follow up on the response, but rather I asked mom what she remembered doing that facilitates leaving one activity to begin the different activity of eating dinner. Mom remembered that she gives Todd a 2-minute warning before the transition. I become excited about the idea and reviewed it with mom, Todd, and dad. They all profess liking this strategy.

Because it was a time of Todd acting responsibly, I return to asking mom what it is like to have Todd act responsibly. Typically the only reason for Todd to cooperate is the positive response he receives from his parents. I want to be certain that both parents understand the importance of their response to Todd's behavior. The positive responses become part of a systemic visualization of the interactions. The visualized rehearsal can create an experience of success and positive affect before the actual behavior occurs. When asked, mom reports really liking Todd's responsible behavior and lists some of his other responsible actions. I paraphrased in an excited manner while smiling at Todd. The father also reported a recent responsible behavior. This was a good sign that dad's new social construction was manifesting itself! I continued focusing upon the positive reports and asked Todd if he knew how proud his mother and dad are that he acts responsibly. Todd responded that he did not know. With a little therapist prompting, Todd's mother and dad told him directly that they are really proud of him while communicating positive emotions. The therapist asked Todd what he likes about responsibility. Todd responded with a non sequitur about not wanting to throw his things away. Perhaps Todd anticipated an unpleasant ending to this conversation!

I asked Todd what his mom does when he acts responsibly. Todd reported that she says thanks. I focused upon the sequence of interactions between Todd and his mother that have to do with Todd acting responsible and his mother responding appreciatively and Todd's enjoyment of his mother's appreciation. I asked Todd what his dad does to show his appreciation. Todd reported that his father does nothing. Todd's father quickly reminded Todd of a time that he said "thank you" recently. This sequence highlights what the family already does to influence one another in helpful ways that engender positive affect. Notice also that the family members are searching their memories for positive behaviors instead of negative ones. This attention to the goal behaviors is ideal in that hope increases and positive feelings are supporting creative solutions.

The initial part of the therapy session focused upon creating neutrality by equal positive attention from me as therapist. You may notice that the other neutrality issue is blame. Initially the blame focused upon Todd's misbehaviors. Lately the blame shifted to father's low rate of sharing positive responses. In the spirit of neutrality, I shifted the focus toward dad's ability as a positive parent. Sensing that the father would like to be viewed more positively, I wanted him to have that opportunity. I used presuppositional language to lead the father into the conversation, asking the father what it is like having Todd act responsibly. After helping the father talk about Todd in proud, positive ways, I asked Todd if he knew that his behavior made his father so happy. Todd reported that he thought his father would just yell at him. I said, "You think your dad would yell at you for doing really good things?"

This interaction eventually lead to several rounds of remembering good things Todd had done and my eliciting proud positive responses from the parents. In session, I attempt to lead overreactions to communicate the importance of the celebrations of success. I asked the family members to imagine the positive interaction sequences and describe what they saw the other person doing as well as self-descriptions. The process is to visualize the sequence and give each person feedback on the expression of support. This usually causes laughter and important reality testing. Most people who have been angry at one another for a while forget how to effectively display their support.

We eventually returned to the shower goal of Todd leaving the 30-minute shower upon request and taking all of the objects out with him. I asked the parents *what it will feel like when they accomplish this goal*. The use of presuppositional language in the question predicts they will accomplish the goal and focuses on the behavior of the parents in maintaining Todd's responsible behavior. Follow-up questions cued the parents to describe their excitement about the specific positive changes that would occur around the shower. Todd was involved by asking him what it will be like to see his parents so excited and happy with him. When I felt certain that he would say yes, I asked him if this is what he wanted as a goal, too. I asked him how it will feel to see his parents so happy with him and he said, "Great." Then I asked the parents if they knew Todd would be this happy and asked them again to describe how happy they would be. Once the mutually beneficial experience of positive emotions was well described and imagined, we returned to the steps of successful showering.

We enacted the shower sequence through our joint visualization. This stepwise process now incorporated their two strengths of giving Todd a 2-minute warning and saying he is number one.

THERAPIST: So I remember earlier that Todd said he was good at cleaning up things for you, mom. Is that how you remember it?

MOM: Yes, I think he does clean up more easily when I ask him to.

THERAPIST: Well, how do you do it? I want to understand!

MOM: I don't know for sure. I ask him and he does it.

THERAPIST: Is that how you see it too, Todd? Mom just asks you and you clean up your stuff?

TODD: Yes, she doesn't yell at me or threaten to throw my collections away.

THERAPIST: I understand, I think. This is like we were talking about earlier. If I or your mom or dad asked you to clean up your collection out of the shower as you leave, in a polite way, you will clean it up. And all these smiles and you're number one will appear? Is that right?

TODD: YES! (Happily imagining the scene.)

THERAPIST: Oh, this is great, Todd! What do you think, mom and dad? Imagine this whole scene. Okay, I look at the clock and notice that there is 2 minutes left of your shower, Todd. So your dad comes to the bathroom and says, Todd, Mr. Number One! You have 2 more minutes in the shower. And what do you do, Todd?

TODD: Nothing. Because I have two more minutes!

THERAPIST: Good! Right! Now dad sees that all of the 30 minutes is gone and he comes back to the shower and says, 'Todd, Mr. Number One! I hope you had a wonderful shower! Please put all of your valuables in the pail so we can save them for later. Todd's number one! Todd's number one!' And what do you do, Todd?

TODD: I turn off the shower and put my things in the pail. And then I say, 'I'm number one!'

THERAPIST: Perfect, Todd! You are number one!! What do you do, dad?

DAD: I smile really big and say with Todd, 'You are number one!!'

THERAPIST: Dad, that is perfect! This is great!

MOM: I'll get you ice cream when you get out of the shower!

THERAPIST: Wow! I never thought of that. What do you think, Todd? You have your dad smiling at you, saying 'Todd's number one,' and your mom getting you ice cream. That is wonderful! Right?

Todd: YES!

Therapist: Mom, what will you do for dad for being such a wonderful guy, too? Would he like a big hug?

Dad: YES!

Therapist: And dad, what will you do for mom for being such a wonderful mom? Would she like a big hug, too?

Mom: That would really be nice!

This continued until the process played out, ending in a small family celebration. I asked them each if this is what they would like their family to be like. And then I mused on how each person is so important in starting the happy process and keeping it alive. By this time, the full responsibility of creating a cooperative, happy family is becoming clear to the parents and dawning upon Todd. Responsibility a la mode!

The visualized rehearsal or role play allowed us to practice the plan ahead of the real homework. Any problems should be encountered while in the session instead of at home. A failure costs at least a week of time and perhaps the family's confidence in family therapy. If I was still uncertain about their ability to implement the homework successfully, I could have asked them to do an actual role play in the session. I could be the movie director getting everyone to stand and move about through the scene. Getting people to overact the positive feelings really makes an impression. Asking if anyone sees a roadblock in our solution can prevent a wasted week. If people doubt each other, I actively support the doubted person and urge him or her to stand up and state he/she will be a successful contributor to the family's success.

Since we arrived at a meta-goal, family happiness, and a subgoal, leaving a clean shower cooperatively, the next step was a miracle question. The miracle question helps cement the understanding of the importance of the subgoal to the major goal as well as the importance of each person in systemic change. Who needs to change first? Anyone and everyone can.

Therapist: I have an interesting question for all of you. It is called a *miracle question*. Do you know what a miracle is?

Todd: Something that you wish for and poof, it is for real.

Therapist: Yes, exactly! A miracle is something that you wish for and poof, it happens. Say this miracle happens tonight, while you are asleep. (Said mysteriously) This miracle happens. But you are asleep so you do not know that it happened! The miracle changes everything that we have talked about. Todd you are really enjoying being responsible!

Todd: That is really a miracle! (Laughing.)

THERAPIST: Yes, a wonderful miracle that changes the whole family! What is the first thing that you notice when you wake up? (Asked to everyone.)

Todd: I would wake up and they wouldn't be yelling at me! (It turns out that waking up in the morning has been a problematic time!)

THERAPIST: Okay, if they are not yelling at you, what do you want them to be doing? You wake up and what are your parents doing?

Todd: I would see mom and dad smiling at me!

THERAPIST: Great! What would you do if you saw them smiling at you?

Todd: I'd smile back!

THERAPIST: What would you do next?

Todd: I'd get out of bed and get dressed right away like they ask me!

Dad: That would be a miracle!

THERAPIST: Wonderful! So, dad, what would you do when you saw Todd smiling, getting up and dressed right away?

Dad: I'd have a big smile on my face and for sure say 'Todd, you are number one!'

THERAPIST: WOW! Show us dad! (Dad demonstrates and Todd erupts with laughter.) Okay, what would happen next? Todd woke up to see dad and mom smiling at him. Todd you smile back at them. (As this is being said I point to them to get them to do it. This solidifies the visualization of the miracle.) Great! And Todd, you hop out of bed and put on your clothes. Dad says . . .

Dad: Todd is number one!

THERAPIST: Great, now what happens?

Mom: We could have cereal together.

This process continues until getting out the door to school. Then we rehearse it one more time. Finally, the miracle was linked back to the family goals and the contributions of each member were reasserted. This process reminded the members that the family depends on each one contributing.

THERAPIST: What if tomorrow, after the miracle tonight, someone forgets to smile? Or forgets to say, 'Todd is number one!' Or forgets to hop out of bed? How can you help each other?

Mom: I can say, 'Where is that beautiful smile Todd?'

THERAPIST: Great! Yes, that is great. Saying what you like is perfect! Saying what you would like from the person is just right! So Todd, if your dad forgets to smile and say you are number one, you could say what?

TODD: DO IT DAD!

THERAPIST: Good. Can you tell him what you like? Can you say, 'Dad I really like it when you smile and say that I'm number one'?'

TODD: Yes, I can do that.

THERAPIST: Great, so let's pretend that dad forgot and you want to remind him. So dad, you play, too.

This sequence helped the family learn to ask for what they wanted from each other, not complain about what they did not like. Being able to respond positively to a request increases positive feelings. Having a flaw pointed out contributes to negative feelings.

THERAPIST: Do you think this miracle would last until shower time at night?

TODD: Yes!

MOM: If it does then we can have ice cream together after your shower!

THERAPIST: Did you hear that, Todd? When you leave the shower on time and pick up your things . . . Wow, when you do that tomorrow, you will get big smiles, 'Todd is number one' and ice cream! Man that will be great!

TODD: Yes!

Next I asked the family two scaling questions. The first question is to imagine a ruler where 0 means, 'not willing to work to make the miracle happen,' and 10 is, 'willing to work very hard.' Todd says he is a 1 or 2. Mother says 9 and father says 8. So I summarized by saying that everyone was willing to work some on the goal.

The second scaling question was to imagine a ruler with 0 meaning, "not hopeful" or that "I do not think this miracle is going to happen." Ten is, "very hopeful, "I believe that this miracle is going to happen." Todd says 8; Mother and Father report a 10. I was very excited about the family's confidence in the miracle. The mother joined in the excitement, stating that there will be more time for Todd to play in the evening once the miracle happens.

I took a break away from the family for 5 minutes to think through the session and decide what homework assignment to give. I knew that I wanted the family to be successful in their homework so the hope and positive feelings that were built in the session have the best chance of increasing. While I was worried that Todd said that he would not put forth much effort, he had been very cooperative and he scaled the occurrence of the miracle at 8, which is very high. I decided to assign the shower task as homework unless Todd reacted negatively during the assignment process.

After the break I complimented the members of the family individually for their willingness to come to counseling and their desire to make the family better. I reviewed the shower sequence with them and linked how each person will be moving toward their larger stated goal through achieving the shower goal. Todd seemed to have forgotten some of the shower process but appeared eager to succeed in the task. I asked mom if she could review the steps with Todd before the shower to help him remember. She and Todd agreed to the addition. Then the first session ended.

First sessions are typically very long—at least 2 hours. This was a good session in that the whole family became invested in the goal and subgoal. If they had not become invested in a workable subgoal the homework task would be the standard first session formula task described in Chapter 2.

TODD'S SECOND SESSION

At the second session, the family revealed that that they did make progress. Three times during the week the shower routine succeeded and two times Todd needed two reminders. The family reported this as a success and that it made bedtime and getting up in the morning much easier. The success called for a therapist soliloquy.

THERAPIST: Isn't it impressive how much he loves you two? He really loves your smiles and praise! This is an amazing family. So much change in just one try! I know that nothing works all the time. There are wonderful days like you guys have had and then some off days. I wish smiles and praise would work every time but I guess nothing works every time. When you have off days I guess you can only walk away shaking your head saying that you'll be glad when your happy Todd comes back! I guess it is hard for us adults to be nice all the time, too!

This tact was to solidify their understanding of the systemic importance of accepting each other's moods or good and bad days with calmness. Typically, we believe that we are entitled to our personal misery and others should not complain. A functional family system will push each member to be energized with positive energy. Some days are off days but there are systemic consequences if the family is not flexible or the off days happen too often.

The second session subgoal was Todd doing his homework. The goal was for him to complete difficult homework confidently and pleasantly with his parents supporting his involvement, focus, and willingness to keep working. Typically, the homework scene involved arguing or complaining with some parental yelling. Neither Todd nor his parents enjoyed homework. Todd did not seem to have coping skills to handle the stress of difficult assignments (a gap in his social skills).

Because all three were pleased with their progress and their relationships, I thought we could introduce a more cognitive intervention. We began by using the exception-finding technique to identify the behavioral or contextual components of the intervention as we had in the first session. When cooperation is low, behavioral strategies provide the best solution. However, cooperation appeared high, so I wanted to introduce coping skills for Todd via modeling.

THERAPIST: When was the last time that doing homework happened just the way y'all liked it?

MOM: Oh, I don't know . . . This last week we had one pretty good evening. Don't you think Todd?

TODD: I don't know.

THERAPIST: What made it a good homework night?

MOM: Well, Todd sat with me in the kitchen and did his homework while I baked cookies.

THERAPIST: So you were in the same room together. Todd was doing his homework. Yippee! (to Todd) . . . and you were baking. *Dad, what were you doing?* (Keeping everyone involved in the family systemic descriptions.)

DAD: Oh, I was reading the paper in the other room.

THERAPIST: Great, so dad, you were doing something quiet, even something similar to Todd's homework in that you were reading, and probably reading the paper was something that Todd did not want to do with you. You think those were the important things?

DAD: Yes, I didn't think of it that way . . .

THERAPIST: Yes, it is hard to know if all of those pieces are important . . . but if it worked once, it might work again! (I want to repeat the ingredients so dad will remember them just in case they are important to success.) So did Todd know that you were in the other room, reading the newspaper?

DAD: Yes, he could see me from the kitchen.

THERAPIST: Wow, it is good you noticed that . . . This could be important. Todd, did you know your dad was in the other room reading while you were doing your homework?

TODD: I don't remember . . .

THERAPIST: Okay . . . Mom, what do you think made the homework evening go so well?

MOM: Well, I know that after supper we all cleaned up the kitchen together and we were all in a good mood.

THERAPIST: You all cleaned up the kitchen together, in a good mood! That is great! Todd, you are very responsible. Helping your parents clean the kitchen! What did you do in the kitchen? You responsible guy!

TODD: I carry the plates, knives, and forks, and glasses from the table to the sink!

THERAPIST: Wow, Todd! That is very responsible of you! Isn't it, dad? Isn't Todd very responsible? The way he helps in the kitchen? (Presuppositional language and catching the child being good . . . in retrospect.)

DAD: Yes, that was responsible.

THERAPIST: Can you tell him that? I bet he'd love to hear it coming from you!

DAD (a little stiff): Todd you were very responsible cleaning up the kitchen.

THERAPIST: Mom? Can you tell Todd, too?

MOM: Of course! Todd, your work in the kitchen was marvelous!

THERAPIST: Wonderful. This is called *catching the child being good*. It means, be on the lookout for anything Todd does that comes close to being responsible in your eyes. When you see it, then be sure to label it as being responsible. That way he feels good about being responsible and he starts to see himself as responsible. His self-concept is growing in the area that you notice and help. It is good to do this in just one area at a time. It seems like his responsibility is most important to you right now. After he is good at that then you can discuss what you would like to be his next virtue or strength to help him develop by noticing and labeling. Does that make sense?

MOM AND DAD: Yes . . .

THERAPIST: You might need to remind each other to keep on the lookout for responsible behavior at first. But soon I'm sure you'll be experts! Cleaning the kitchen with you, his showering, his homework . . . lots of things. If you don't notice it right away, maybe you can remember them at suppertime to tell Todd about his responsible behavior then! Make responsibility something he becomes confident in and feels good about.

DAD: I really like that idea!

THERAPIST: Oops, I changed the topic, didn't I, Todd! . . . We were talking about making homework a better time! Maybe even happy! (Laughing) So we talked about dad reading in the next room and the enjoyable, responsible, clean-up time together after supper. Now how did you get the homework started?

MOM: I'm not sure. I usually just say go get your books . . . but then usually Todd disappears and I have to go drag him into the kitchen . . .

THERAPIST: So it would be best to have his books in the kitchen? Is that what you're suggesting?

MOM: No, we have a small kitchen and too much clutter already.

THERAPIST: Oh, good point. (Never disagree with the customer if you can help it.) Maybe dad could bring the books into the kitchen when he gets the newspaper to read?

DAD: Well, yes, I could do that.

THERAPIST: Is that okay with you Todd? (Neutrality, keeping everyone involved and invested.) We could get your dad working for you carrying the books!

TODD: Yeah! Make him work too!!

DAD: Oh NOOO! (Getting into the spirit of fun now.)

THERAPIST: Wonderful! Dad is being responsible. Just like Todd! Okay. We have a cleaned-up kitchen that everyone is being responsible for and happy about! Remember to stay happy while you clean so homework is good, too! (This is more a reminder for dad than Todd!) We have dad working hard carrying the books before he does his homework of reading the paper. Next I'd like to try something new if it's okay with you guys . . .

I asked Todd to tell us about the best part of doing his homework. It took a bit of work to uncover any positive aspect. Finding joy in homework can be difficult for a child. The next day at school is often the time that completing homework feels good. For Todd, the next day is a good feeling because he gets to show the teacher his finished work, see her happy, and feel proud of his work. When he has not turned in homework he is embarrassed. We used his successful mental images to frame helpful, supportive self-talk for him to use as encouragement as he begins his homework. I asked his mom to coach him through this process in the evening. This is teaching him a coping skill of getting through less pleasant tasks for a delayed reward.

Mom was asked to coach Todd in the session so I can help with the process. She is to tell Todd that sometimes parts of homework can be very difficult but if he keeps trying, he figures it out. Todd is number one! And then he can think of his teacher the next day looking at his work and giving him a big smile. Then he feels wonderful pride. She is to remind Todd to feel really good about how hard he worked and how wonderful he can feel to have worked so hard. I really wanted him to feel good about working hard. When mom and Todd have worked through the coaching of Todd's coping and positive self-talk training, I asked dad to be involved in the enactment. Dad acted like he was getting the books and encouraging Todd as well.

The time for consulting with Todd's teacher seemed right by the second session. I got a release from the family to call Todd's teacher to tell her about the progress we were making. When I called Todd's teacher I told her how important she was in Todd's life. I added that Todd had been saying that he really wants to please her. So we worked this week on getting better at doing his homework. I let her know that she could really help if she would be ready to smile really big and make a fuss over his completed homework. I told her that I cannot guarantee that he will complete his homework but her help would be really important. Todd's teacher was very willing to help. Requesting a teacher to help in this manner has never failed.

Todd's Third Session

The third session was 2 weeks after the second. At the beginning of the third session the family reported that the homework goals were met and there was generally more cooperation and enjoyment. Also, Todd reported that his parents behaved better, thus, showing progress in their goals of reminding, encouraging, and praising him. Beyond the session goals, the parents noted that Todd asked for flashcards to help him learn and was generally more motivated. Todd also decreased his gathering of objects and began to throw away some of the previously gathered objects. We had never discussed this as a goal or specifically as a problem since the first session when his collections were described. Todd was helping around the house, and the school noted that his reading level was improving. The third session goal was to complete spelling worksheets cooperatively and for his parents to show pride in him. I also introduced a goal of having family friends over. This was not an easy topic but finally mom could think of a family that had a child close to Todd's age that they would invite over. We visualized a successful visit during the session.

TODD'S FOURTH SESSION

Two weeks later at the fourth session Todd's parents reported that he was happier, had improved his reading skills, had gotten a positive note from school, cleaned-up more, and was completing reading worksheets and finishing homework independently.

They did not visit with the friends but promised it would happen before the next session. We enacted a telephone invitation in session. Each member of the family pretended to call me on the phone to invite me over to the house. The fourth session goal was to maintain or increase positive interactions in the family and consider what organizations Todd could join for social contact. Both parents seemed more open to Todd's sociability than their own.

TODD'S FIFTH SESSION

Two weeks later, at the fifth session, Todd brought an award from school announcing his achievement in reading and science. Todd's parents reported less frequent arguments with Todd and that Todd negotiated well when disagreements happened. Todd would be going to a local boys club meeting the next week that focused on cooperative athletic events and cooperative board games. The parents promised to research the games and play them at home as well. Throughout the session the parents' goal was to improve their reminding, encouraging, and praising behaviors. They did this well. The parents were beginning to understand the importance of social involvement as well. Todd reported his parent's continuous improvement.

Counseling was terminated by mutual decision at the fifth session. The family members reported reaching their goals and being satisfied with the family therapy. Todd voiced the only concern. He worried that his dad may not continue his new positive behavior.

At the 3-month follow-up the parents and Todd reported that things were continuing to go well. The parents reported that their relationship with Todd had continued to improve. Todd had joined the local boys club and his experiences at school continued to improve.

Careful readers of this case may wonder why the family did not work on one of the initial presenting problems—cruelty to a family cat. Children who purposefully and repeatedly hurt animals are in a high-risk group for serious emotional and behavioral problems. Hearing about animal cruelty is a red flag for therapists. In this case, the incident appeared to be isolated, Todd was clearly hungry for adult attention, and I imagined that the incident had something to do with his own pet parrot's interaction with the cat. If, however, evidence of chronic cruelty had been available, some family goal for responsible care of pets would have been established.

CASE 2: HUGS AND TEARS

Mrs. Vasquez brought her daughter, Yolanda, to family therapy because Yolanda cried upon going to fifth grade. Mrs. Vasquez had separated from her husband during the summer. Yolanda was born in the United States. Mrs. Vasquez was born in Mexico and came to the United States about 15 years ago. Her partner was born in the United States but 3 months ago left the state to pursue another career or another relationship—Mrs. Vasquez was not certain which. Mrs. Vasquez and Yolanda are bilingual (Spanish and English). Mrs. Vasquez has a brother with a family who lives in her neighborhood, but the rest of her family including her mother and father live in central Mexico. Visitation is difficult and so they rarely see the extended family.

RECORD OF INITIAL MEETING

As I meet Mrs. Vasquez I am aware that she is of Mexican ancestry and I am of Scottish ancestry. I have a long cultural past of my family living in the United States for many generations as part of the majority culture. Mrs. Vasquez does not. Her culture is likely to be influenced by her Mexican heritage. We are likely to have differences even though we both now live in a state that borders Mexico and has benefited from the acculturative contributions of the location.

One issue that I wish to address in the initial encounter is *formalismo*. That is, I wish to match Mrs. Vasquez's social conventions. Because this will be our initial meeting, I will treat her with great respect (*respecto*)—as a woman of status would be treated in Mexico. She is likely to be more acculturated than my preparations presume, but I plan to be safe. I wish to be a little more formal in my dress and salutations than I normally am with new clients, at least initially. I wish to convey my respect for her and her daughter based upon my assumption that Mrs. Vasquez has experienced the pain of racism from people who look like me, members of the majority culture. I would like to indirectly communicate my respect for her position in life—an adult woman who is a mother of an 11-year-old daughter and is working hard to make a good life for her daughter despite the fact that she is on her own. I suspect that if Mrs. Vasquez views me as a racist person, who views her and her daughter as less worthy or less able than White, non-Hispanic people (as the census describes us), she will benefit less from family therapy and suffer another micro-aggression of racism.

THERAPIST: Mrs. Vasquez, thank you so much for coming! I'm Dr. Conoley, Collie Conoley. I appreciate your coming today. How do you like to be addressed? As Mrs. or Ms. Lopez, or de Vasquez, or Mrs. Vasquez?

MRS. VASQUEZ: It is good to meet you. Please call me Mrs. Vasquez.

THERAPIST: And this must be Yolanda! Much gusto conocerte, Yolanda.

MRS. VASQUEZ: *¿Habla Español, doctor?*

THERAPIST: Un poquito. Que lastima! (Everyone laughs.) I have taken many years of Spanish but I really am very bad, I'm sorry to say. I very much admire your ability to be bilingual. One day I hope to be! You also have a broader experience than I. I have lived in only one country, while you understand at least two cultures very well. Please, have a seat Mrs. Vasquez and Yolanda. I am so pleased that you are here. (I hope this conversation signals my admiration of Mrs. Vasquez's language ability and the benefit she has of having lived in Mexico. Also, it opens the door for me to ask for cultural clarifications if I do not understand or for her to correct me if I misperceive.)

MRS. VASQUEZ: Thank you.

THERAPIST: May I get you anything to drink?

MRS. VASQUEZ: No, thank you.

YOLANDA: No, thank you.

THERAPIST: Have you been to family therapy before?

MRS. VASQUEZ: No . . .

THERAPIST: Let me tell you about family therapy then. Family therapy is a way to help each person in the family reach his or her goals using the strength of the family. Family therapy helps the family help the person or more than one person who is having problems. In family therapy, I will help you decide how you want things to be—that is, help you think of your goals and then help you accomplish your goals. Is this okay? (Providing initial structure removes some of the initial anxiety.)

MRS. VASQUEZ: Yes.

THERAPIST: Yolanda, is this okay for you, too? (Neutrality, however I address mom first in matching cultural suppositions that I have, thus far.)

YOLANDA: Yes . . .

THERAPIST: The first step in family therapy is that I would like to get to know each of you a little better. I want to know about you so that I can understand your strengths, what you are good at doing, what you enjoy doing. That way, when it comes time to figure out how to reach your goals, I can help you use your strengths to accomplish your goals—using what you do best to reach your goals. So at first I'll just ask about you, then I will ask you about what you would like to accomplish in family therapy, and finally I will help you figure out how to accomplish your goals. How does that sound to you? (I structure the beginning session with a great deal of information about family therapy for families that have not been in therapy before. I am careful to explain why I am asking personal questions about each member and I will remind them often through the process, especially if I notice discomfort or hesitation. I hope talking initially in a friendly manner will give the family members time to relax and feel more comfortable with the setting.)

MRS. VASQUEZ: That sounds fine.

THERAPIST: Do you have any questions about me or family therapy?

MRS. VASQUEZ: Yes, how long will this take?

THERAPIST: That is a very good question. Most of the time I see families anywhere from 5 to 10 sessions. It depends on how big the goals are and how quickly we can reach our goals. Sometimes we get started on a big goal and after meeting a few times the family feels that things are going so well they can get to the goal without meeting with me. If they get stuck later they could come back. Is that okay with you?

MRS. VASQUEZ: Yes, 5 or so sessions seems fine. How often will we meet and do you need me here? (This may represent a common cultural deference to believe the doctor will fix the problem, not the parent.)

THERAPIST: Oh yes! You are very important to Yolanda's growth. And I want to be certain that you are involved in choosing the important goals. Also, I will meet with you once a week or later we will probably meet every other week, every 2 weeks. So you will be able to help Yolanda everyday but I will see her only once a week or once every 2 weeks.

MRS. VASQUEZ: Oh, okay.

THERAPIST: Yolanda, is this okay with you as well? Is it okay that your mom comes each time? (I knew that Yolanda would absolutely want her mom to come! I hope that asking what Yolanda wants will help her feel more comfortable with the process by having some control over it.)

YOLANDA: YES! I want mama here.

THERAPIST: Great, any other questions for me? Anytime you have questions please ask, okay? Well, Yolanda, what do you like to do for fun?

I ask Yolanda about her activities after school, on weekends, and what she enjoys at school. She is shy, very polite, and a good student. She has two close girl friends at school and spends afternoons and weekends with her next-door cousins, whom she enjoys. She likes her teacher and believes her teacher likes her. She enjoys electronic games, television, and art. She appears to be able to follow through on projects and concentrate well. She made no mention of her father.

Mrs. Vasquez works at a grocery store from 10 AM until 8 PM. She has worked there for 10 years and enjoys the work environment. She has taken community college classes in English and business. She would like to become a bookkeeper for local businesses. She socializes with her friends from work and her relatives who live nearby. She tells me that Yolanda's father left 4 months ago. She thinks he left the state and will not come back. Both Yolanda and Mrs. Vasquez are in tears as the father's story gets told.

THERAPIST: I can see that his leaving is very painful for both of you. Do you feel the pain often?

MRS. VASQUEZ: I don't like for Yolanda to see me cry but I cry nearly every night when I go to bed.

THERAPIST: You feel the pain every night. That is difficult. Why don't you like for Yolanda to see you cry?

MRS. VASQUEZ: She is having so many difficulties. I don't want to make her feel worse seeing me cry. (Mrs. Vasquez is crying and Yolanda begins to cry more.)

THERAPIST: I can see how much you love Yolanda. That is wonderful that you love her so much and want a good life for her.

MRS. VASQUEZ: Yes . . .

THERAPIST: Yolanda, did you know how much your mother loves you?

YOLANDA: Yes.

THERAPIST: Did you know she hides her tears from you?

YOLANDA: No.

THERAPIST: Yolanda, do you hide your tears from your mother?

YOLANDA: Yes, I don't want to make her cry.

THERAPIST: You love your mother a lot, don't you. Yolanda? And you want her to have a good life, too? Yes?

YOLANDA: Yes . . . (Crying more. And her mother hugging her.)

THERAPIST: What a wonderful family. So much love and caring. What a wonderful family. (Mrs. Vasquez seems to change as she hears an evaluation of her family as wonderful. Her experience may be that she failed her family because her husband has left.)

THERAPIST: Mrs. Vasquez, what a wonderful mother you are. I see you comforting Yolanda in her pain. And Yolanda, what a wonderful daughter you are. You comfort your mother, hoping that her pain will go away. (They stop crying and laugh somewhat in embarrassment.) Did that feel good? To cry together?

MRS. VASQUEZ (with a self-conscious giggle): Yes.

THERAPIST: So you were very sad and with hugs and crying together, now you are better?

MRS. VASQUEZ: Yes.

THERAPIST: And for you, Yolanda? Do you feel better after crying and hugging your mom?

YOLANDA: Yes, I do . . .

THERAPIST: That is a wonderful skill that you both have. Isn't it? You can cry and hug; then you feel better.

MRS. VASQUEZ AND YOLANDA (looking at each other): Yes . . .

THERAPIST: Maybe you don't need to hide your tears? Just ask for a hug?

As a therapist I merely observed that after they cried and hugged, they appeared to feel better. They confirmed my observation and seemed embarrassed about crying but pleased about their experience. Their ability to comfort each other was clearly a strength.

THERAPIST: I can see that thinking about Yolanda's dad makes both of you sad. How would you like to feel when you think about him?

MRS. VASQUEZ: What do you mean?

THERAPIST: Well, when my dad died, at first I cried a lot and felt like a big part of my life was gone. But now, I sometimes feel sad. I'll cry when I remember him but most of the time I remember the nice things we did together. I try to remember that even though I'll never see him again, he has left me with many wonderful memories. Has anything like that happened for either of you?

MRS. VASQUEZ: Yes, I was very close to my grandmother in Mexico. When she died I was very sad. My mother and I cried and cried. But Raul did not die. He left.

THERAPIST: And that is more difficult. You don't know whether he will come back? And your grandmother didn't want to die but Raul did choose to leave? Is that the difference?

MRS. VASQUEZ: Yes . . .

THERAPIST: How would you like to think of Raul? How would you like Yolanda to remember her father?

MRS. VASQUEZ: Well, I know that it is not good for Yolanda to have bad thoughts about her father. But I know he hurt me and I'm angry with him.

THERAPIST: He hurt you. He hurt you badly. How will you feel when the hurting stops?

MRS. VASQUEZ: Oh, I see what you mean . . . I guess I feel really ashamed, too. I don't want to feel hurt or ashamed. But I did not come here for me. I want Yolanda to feel better.

THERAPIST: You are right. Yolanda should feel better. (Agree with the customer.) That is why you don't want her to see your pain or tears.

MRS. VASQUEZ: That is right.

THERAPIST: It is strange, though . . . I don't understand it, but when you talked about your pain, cried, and held Yolanda, she felt better. You helped her feel better. Right?

MRS. VASQUEZ: Yes . . . Is that right Yolanda?

YOLANDA: Yes . . . (Yolanda giggles and her mother smiles.)

THERAPIST: It seems that we need to help both of you know how to help each other. Yolanda, are you happier when your mom is happy?

YOLANDA: Yes!

THERAPIST: And your mom really wants you to be happy too, Yolanda.

YOLANDA: Yes.

THERAPIST: So let's focus on your mom's concern. She wants you to be happier going to school. Is that right, Mrs. Vasquez?

MRS. VASQUEZ: Yes.

THERAPIST: Is that okay with you, Yolanda? Would you like to be happier going to school?

YOLANDA: Yes, but when I'm at school I miss mama. (She bites her lip to keep from crying and trembles.)

MRS. VASQUEZ: And she is not eating breakfast. She says she is not hungry. And she wears a jacket to school because she gets cold. . . . In this heat, a jacket! I think she is nervous . . . anxious.

THERAPIST: Do you think your mom is right, Yolanda? Do you feel nervous? Jumpy? Like little things will upset you?

YOLANDA: Yes.

THERAPIST: What do you do to get over it? Is there any time when those bad feelings are gone?

YOLANDA: Yes, they are gone when I'm playing with my friends or during art time at school.

THERAPIST: So when you are having fun with your friends or fun at art, you feel the way you like to feel?

YOLANDA: Yes.

THERAPIST: So that is good. You know that having fun makes the nervous feelings go away. Sometimes when one parent leaves, we worry that the other parent might leave, too. Do you think that your mom might leave?

YOLANDA (with a little panic in her voice): NO!

THERAPIST: Good. Mrs. Vasquez, is that true? Are you going to leave Yolanda?

MRS. VASQUES: No. I would never leave Yolanda.

THERAPIST: That is what I thought. Tell Yolanda that. Tell her and let's see if it helps.

MRS. VASQUES: Yolanda, you know that I'll never leave you. (Yolanda starts to cry.)

THERAPIST: Yolanda, how does it feel to hear you mom say that she will never leave you? Does that feel good or bad?

YOLANDA: Good . . . It feels good.

THERAPIST: When your mom tells you that she will always be close by, she will always be here for you, that makes you feel better? (Notice the slight change to frame the issue into the positive.)

YOLANDA: Yes.

THERAPIST: So our goal is to help you feel calm and confident that you can count on your mother. Your mother will be with you. Is that a good goal for us?

YOLANDA: Yes.

MRS. VASQUEZ: Yes.

THERAPIST: Good! We have an important goal! Yolanda, we want you to feel calm and confident about your mom at school, at home, I guess everywhere.

At this point I want to know what aspects of Yolanda's relationship with her mom are most salient. She has a wonderful memory of her mom combing her hair and their shopping together. Using her most powerful images or memories of being with her mom will be used in helping Yolanda learn self-soothing skills. Yolanda enjoys art, so I ask Yolanda to draw a picture about each image. After she draws the pictures I ask her to think about what she would like to say to herself when she looks at the pictures. She says that she will remind herself how her mother and she will have fun. I ask Yolanda to rehearse using the pictures. She laughs and follows through well.

This went so well that I ask Yolanda to think of things at school that she enjoys the most. Then I ask her to draw pictures of the two activities at school. She will hang these pictures up at home to look at before going to school. She will remind herself that she has fun at school and with her mom. She has them both!

Yolanda knew how to distract herself from the fear of losing her mom by using activities such as playing with her friends. But distraction from a dreaded thought cannot continuously work. That would be a negative coping style of avoidance. I wanted her to feel comfortable, however, being able to allow her mind to wander or relax without fear of a dreaded thought. Having tools to directly counter the feared thoughts should erode their power. If the pictures and self-statements worked, Yolanda would have a tool at her disposal to invoke helpful thoughts and feelings. When her feelings or thoughts experienced a negative state, she would know how to soothe herself.

Similarly, because Mrs. Vasquez did not want to address the loss of her husband, the only avenue to help Mrs. Vasquez was through helping Yolanda. Hearing her mom cry in the evening troubled Yolanda. Sharing tears, hugs, and positive statements could be reassuring for both people.

I took a 5-minute break to think through the events of the session. Both mother and daughter seemed willing to work on the issues that brought them to therapy. Mrs. Vasquez did not wish to focus on her husband's departure. I honored her wish.

THERAPIST: I am so pleased to meet both of you. Thank you so much for coming to see me. I am honored. I have enjoyed getting to know both of you. I know that both of you have a difficult loss to cope with when your father, your husband left. I am deeply sorry that he left. I know that you came to see me so that Yolanda, you, could be happier going to school. Your mother wants you to enjoy life as much as possible. Your mother wants you to be very happy. . . . And I know you want your mother to be very happy, too!

We learned a very helpful thing today. We learned that if you cry together and hug each other for just a couple of minutes it makes you both feel better. Since you both want each other to feel better and you both do feel better when you cry and hug for a few minutes, I would like you to do that every night this week. I would like to add one thing to the cry and hug. When you are finished hugging, think about something that you noticed that the other person did that you liked that day and tell her. Okay?

BOTH: Yes.

THERAPIST: Let's act this scene out in our minds. So, which room do you imagine you will hug in?

MRS. VASQUEZ: Your bedroom.

THERAPIST: Okay, you both are in the bedroom. Who will say 'let's hug and cry'?

YOLANDA: You say it, mama.

MRS. VASQUEZ: Okay, I'll say it.

THERAPIST: So what will you say, Mrs. Vasquez?

MRS. VASQUEZ: I'll say time to hug, Yolanda! (I notice that the crying is not included.)

THERAPIST: Great, so you'll say 'Time to hug and cry, Yolanda!' Is it okay if Yolanda comes into your bedroom to ask you for a hug and cry if you forget, Mrs. Vasquez?

MRS. VASQUEZ: Yes.

THERAPIST: Will you do that, Yolanda? I know you want your mom to be happy!

YOLANDA: Yes, I'll do it.

THERAPIST: Great! Then you each have to think of something that the other person did that day that you liked and tell them. It is like a compliment. So what is something that Yolanda did today that you liked, Mrs. Vasquez? Tell her what you liked.

MRS. VASQUEZ: Hmm. Yolanda, I thought you looked beautiful today! I thought your hair was nice.

THERAPIST: Wonderful! Did you like that Yolanda, being noticed by your mom? What is something you noticed that your mom did today that you liked?

YOLANDA: I like it that you hugged me! That felt good.

THERAPIST: Wonderful! Y'all are really good at this!

So the other part is hanging Yolanda's pictures of school up at home so she can look at them every morning when she is going to leave.

MRS. VASQUEZ: I think we should put them in the car. That is where she gets sad.

THERAPIST: Great idea. That is much better!

YOLANDA: I'll put the other pictures of mom and me on my notebook. It has a plastic liner.

THERAPIST: Great! Another great idea! So that is your homework. Could you review it again for me, Yolanda? What are you going to do?

Yolanda remembers everything. So we set an appointment for next week.

YOLANDA'S SECOND SESSION

At the second session, Mrs. Vasquez and Yolanda arrive with news of success. While they didn't cry every day, they did cry twice during the week; they hugged every night. They enjoyed saying something they noticed about each other and laughed as they recounted a remembrance. Mrs. Vasquez reported that Yolanda ate breakfast every morning except one and did not cry on the way to school at all. Yolanda forgot what to say to herself but she said looking at the pictures helped. Also, her mom drew a picture of a heart for her and wrote "I love you" across it. Yolanda loved that addition.

When asked what else they would like to accomplish, they declined to have another goal. I told them that I enjoyed working with them and asked them to call if they wanted future services. They achieved what they sought in family therapy. I trust that the growth toward their goals will continue moving them in a direction of escalating betterment, of broadening and building (Fredrickson, 1998).

These two examples provide an integration of the primary techniques from the previous chapters. Unfortunately, not every idea presented in the previous chapters is demonstrated in the case examples. The written transcripts are abbreviated and edited to make the sessions as helpful as possible. Our brilliant students deserve a great deal of credit for the content of these examples.

CHAPTER 5

Wrap Up and Future Directions

GOAL OF CHAPTER 5

Positive approaches to therapy have attracted criticism and misunderstanding. These are raised in this chapter with some comment. In addition, future research agendas and issues around termination are introduced.

Key concepts: cultural competence, generalization of treatment gains, goal setting, termination, trauma writing.

INTRODUCTION

Several bodies of research and clinical work inform Positive Family Therapy, including a variety of family systems theories (e.g., Smith, Ingoldsby, Miller, & Hamon, 2008; White & Klein, 2007), especially *Solution Focused Therapy*. In addition, research from the recently emerging *Positive Psychology* movement has been incorporated (e.g., Seligman et al., 2005) with well-documented strategies from *Cognitive Behavioral Therapy* (e.g., Beck, 1975; Hollon & Beck, 2004; Linehan, 1993) and findings from the child development and experimental personality literature (e.g., Fredrickson, Tugade, Waugh, & Larkin, 2003; Tronick, 1989).

Science and practice are moving very quickly in the study of human behavior. In particular, breakthroughs in neuroscience illustrate how brain structure and function affect and are affected by behavior (e.g., Sapolsky, 2004). Further, evidence from positive psychology and public health indicate the close relationship of emotion to indexes of health (e.g., Davidson & Kabat-Zin, 2003).

Thus, it seems clear that positive therapeutic approaches to families and individuals as a treatment of choice will increase in quantity and quality based on energetic research. Our initial attempt at synthesis in this volume will undoubtedly require continuous updating. In this last chapter, some of these next steps are mentioned.

URGENT RESEARCH AGENDAS

The goal of positive psychology is human flourishing (Gable & Haidt, 2005)—so, too, the goal of Positive Family Therapy. Each member of a family must be helped to attain optimal functioning. The analogous processes of *escalation* and *broaden and build* describe the reciprocal growth of skills and positive emotions. This spiral of interaction of affect, behavior, and cognition within the open system holds the promise of development, but it depends on continual attention and effort. Families, frustrated by years of failure with each other, often approach therapy with the hope that one member can be dropped off and fixed. The initial session in Positive Family Therapy engages family members in the process and renews underused positive feelings. Strategies to involve everyone in the process of therapy are well developed and successful in creating therapeutic alliances that scaffold change. Families must leave therapy, however, knowing that continuous growth requires hard work for a lifetime. Fortunately, the effort invested in relationships yields positive, mutually enhancing experiences. Motivating families to persist in effortful change—that is, *generalize* the treatment gains to new settings and across time—is a significant challenge that demands research and clinical investigation. Motivation must be matched with skills that change as the family develops, children grow up and leave, and parents age. Our current model of mental health service is not a good match to this lifetime framework. We do not think of therapy in the same way we think about dental checkups, but perhaps we should.

A central aspect of Positive Family Therapy is the strong focus on goal setting as a primary path toward health and growth (Gable, 2008). Therapists strive to respect each family member's goal, but not all family member goals are consistent with positive family values. Some members enjoy doing things or are good at some things (our usual definition of *strengths*) that are antisocial. Thus, some families are not sources of strength, safety, and development, but they are rather arenas of abuse and neglect. Although ethically and morally we strive to save every life (e.g., threatened by suicide), we do not experience the same moral or ethical demands to save every family. Evidence of child, spousal, or elder abuse may force us to act in ways that actually contribute to the dissolution of a family. Family connections exert a primary influence on all members, however, and these influences are not easily or predictably constructed outside of the family. There is a tremendous need for research, theory, and resources to construct secure and enhancing living arrangements that replicate the best parts of family life for those whose families of origin fall short of being safe havens for them.

Investigating family member goals sometimes uncovers levels of personal sacrifice that members are making that seem out of proportion to reasonable expectations. Obviously, the individual's perspective and the family culture both require respectful investigation to scale the therapists' perceptions of sacrifice. Extreme sacrifices, even freely chosen, should be examined openly with that person to spotlight the balance of sacrifice to family benefit. Most relationships provide some benefits, but as family therapists we need to focus attention on the inequitable benefits and sacrifices individuals make in families. Common examples of this are women and men who endure psychological abuse or the traumas associated with a partner's addictions in order to save the family.

Some sacrifices are less dramatic but equally worthy of elevation to overt processing. Oppressive gender roles may trap both sexes in constrained lives that seem blocked and stagnant. The powerful influences of gender stereotypes, culture, religion, and tradition may support these narrow niches of life. Family therapists who strive toward high levels of cultural competence need continuous upgrades in their information, affect, and values to navigate these situations ethically and effectively. Current best practice suggests development of negotiated goals that rely on family values to facilitate culturally informed goals. These goals are sometimes unsatisfying when measured against human potential for optimal functioning and flourishing. Although there is a fairly large extant multicultural literature to consult, this remains an area in urgent need of improved research designs and evidence (Gushue, Greenan, & Brazaitis, 2005).

Finally, a common positive psychology assignment is to have individuals reflect on and write down things about which they are grateful (e.g., Emmons & McCullough, 2003). There is also a persuasive body of literature that illustrates the efficacy of writing about trauma (e.g., Pennebaker, 1997). The relative usefulness of these strategies deserves some direct test. Reviews of the trauma writing suggest that a link among emotional expression, cognitive restructuring, and behavioral change may be a driver of improvements in physical symptoms (e.g., reduced colds, improved sleep, better immune functioning, fewer doctor visits). Further study is warranted to investigate if these findings are well explained by the broaden-and-build perspective or if they represent another avenue for alleviating individual distress (Cohn, Mehl, & Pennebaker, 2004; Fredrickson et al., 2003).

MISUNDERSTANDING POSITIVE FAMILY THERAPY

The integration of positive psychology with family therapy may be dismissed as lacking the necessary complexity demanded by the many layers of family history and dynamics. A common misunderstanding of positive psychology is that it is simple minded. Perhaps the most-noted nonscholarly criticism is Stuart Smalley's (a.k.a., celebrity Al Franken) presentation of therapy: *"I'm good enough; I'm smart enough; and doggone it, people like me"* (Franken, 1992). We laugh along with Franken as he presents Stuart Smalley's multiple issues—issues he fails to remedy with a simplistic self-affirmation or the use of other aphorisms. Were we Mr. Smalley's family therapists, we would support his self-affirmations and then move on to some other important goals. The caricature of therapy Mr. Smalley presents does us a service, however, in summarizing the harshest criticism of our approach.

The most underrated skill in Positive Family Therapy is therapeutic goal setting. Many novice therapists, eager to help clients feel better immediately, attempt to deny or minimize the problem the client experiences. Often this occurs with the statement similar to, "Oh, you're not that bad," or, "I have had that problem, only worse!" An analysis of the beginning therapist's helpfulness could be: "Here's a short cut. The goal can be a denial of the problem." Upon reflection, two issues become clear: Most clients have already tried and failed at denial; and then there is the important existential issue that human growth is constantly precipitated by overcoming difficulties as well as by celebrating success. Positive Family Therapy does not promote denial. Difficulties are a message to hear—understanding that change may be needed. The goal of change is not embedded in the relief of pain. Increased positive feeling and less frequent emotional pain are signs of progress. A high-functioning life is not based on pain avoidance but on approaching meaningful goals.

Thinking—a basic engine of human growth—is both friend and foe of happiness. Common wisdom is confusing. Consider well-known aphorisms: "She who hesitates is sometimes lost"; "Look before you leap."

Clients like Todd from Chapter 4 need assistance in cognitive coping skills. They must be motivated to establish cognitive goals that include anticipating the consequences of their actions, affirming their abilities to do difficult things, reinforcing their attempts to complete assignments, and noticing the positive behaviors of others. Todd did learn to "look before he leapt," but the process of doing so is complex and highly nuanced by his family situation and personal history.

Other clients present with well-developed thought–action patterns. They are not impulsive and are sensitive and empathic to the situations of others. They are, however, suffering from their strengths of analysis and empathy. Chapter 4's Yolanda was hurt by her father's abandonment and acutely aware of her mother's sadness. She "got" the situation and it made her highly anxious.

Assisting clients to think in more helpful ways is central to many therapeutic goals; however, goal selection with anxiety disorders requires careful consideration. First, goals for people experiencing anxiety must be proximal to their issues. They need a new strategy to cope with their felt needs. Several therapeutic tactics reduce anxiety—for example, exposure, relaxation, and cognitive restructuring. Matching some enactment of these to a client's goals is delicate, however, because clients, like Yolanda, may say they want to forget or stop thinking about traumatic events—that is, avoid the thoughts or memory as much as possible. The second challenge is discerning the most proximal problem. Is it fearing the memory or remembering the event? The two formulations lead to different goals. Does the memory need to be reinterpreted or does the client need new skills in coping with the trauma. For example, the therapist could strive to help a child or rejected wife think, "It is better that dad left. If he had stayed he would have been miserable and probably made us miserable, too. I disagree with what he did but maybe he did not think it through well and understand what he did." The memory of abandonment gets shifted to a memory of dad making a very poor and uninformed decision. It becomes about his failing, not the child's or the wife's shortcomings.

As a contrast or complement to this goal, a client may need a functional way of coping with the current interpretation of the memory. That is, the memory (e.g., "I've been abandoned") is not adjusted, but the fear associated with it is mitigated because attention is shifted to a coping strategy. For example, the goal, "We will hug each other and cry. Then we feel better. The sting of the memory will always be there but not as strong. Nothing is to be feared from remembering this because we have each other." This approach remembers the trauma but is dedicated to lessoning the pain that the memory brings based on the power of social support.

Both processes may be useful—helping clients revise some memories and acknowledge the full import of others. The meta-goal, of course, is to allow clients to experience their lives fully in the present with at least the hope that past memories are not overshadowed by particularly traumatic events but are differentiated into good and bad times. Flourishing requires awareness and openness to the joys of present and future relationships, not avoiding the risks of involvement.

Extreme examples of the past overshadowing the present, for example, in clients suffering from Posttraumatic Stress Disorder, illustrate the complex therapeutic tasks associated with helping clients find strategies (i.e., commit to goals) to alleviate anxiety. Family goals in such cases must include developing individual and relationship plans to comfort the traumatized family member. Individual goals must be crafted so the client comes to recognize signs that a memory, not the present moment, is precipitating a particular feeling. Coping with the past trauma and present stressors becomes a focus. Clients must learn tactics to reduce fear, increase hope, and to analyze (or at least attend to) current interactions with a commitment to seek positive interpretations. This is a very tall order for everyone involved in the therapeutic relationship.

In addition to criticisms that positive approaches are too simple to be useful is the historical context of mental health intervention. The history of psychotherapy is heavily weighted toward explorations of serious dysfunction (e.g., Schizophrenia, depression, anxiety, aggression, psychosis, and sociopathy). Our own work has brought us into contact with serious mental illness and flagrant examples of evil. Theories to explain and strategies to ameliorate these behaviors are naturally shaped by the presenting symptoms and cultural contexts. Many of the symptoms are scary and reveal humans as confused, hopeless, and dangerous. Some practitioners may have difficulty believing that positive strategies are powerful enough to manage these extreme symptoms.

In addition, health care in the twenty-first century is informed by 100 years of advances in life and physical sciences that have improved medical and pharmaceutical treatments at exponential rates. The map of the human genome is known and applications of this knowledge are just on the horizon. The propensity to look toward psychopharmacological treatments, especially, as primary avenues for psychological and behavior change is very strong. It seems difficult to believe that people through persistent cognitive effort and emotional control can change, not only their thoughts, behaviors, and feelings, but also their body chemistry, their relationships, and their communities. Some people seem too "sick" and medicine seems much stronger than psychological effort. Positive approaches can seem soft, unscientific, and strangely "spiritual" in the face of enormous challenges. Drugs clearly have improved the life options for thousands of people with serious mental illness. Their use, however, as a replacement for persistent efforts to restructure cognitions and increase positive affect is not yet warranted by the research.

Healthy skepticism is always the friend of progress, however. Combinations of approaches are likely in the future to be most ameliorative for clients—combinations that include the talk therapy outlined in this volume with medical and genetic support as needed. The quality of human life as being always in action with others and always developing unique meanings about these interactions suggests that persistent psychological effort will also always be needed for happy family life.

Finally, two world wars, numerous regional wars, ongoing genocidal campaigns, hovering threats of terrorist attacks, and continuous reports of greed, corruption, and incompetence among world leaders reveal a side of human behavior that, while understandable to some degree, is nonetheless far from positive. It is tempting to see positive psychologists as out of touch with reality. We prefer to see ourselves as enacting the changes necessary for family and world peace and widespread compassion despite history of human failure.

FAMILY GROWTH

Setting goals for family growth can be daunting. Parents bring their children to family therapy to benefit the children. Seldom does the parent consider or easily accept a goal of self-growth. Often, however, children's mental health mirrors their parents' functioning. When this mirroring issue is framed from a deficit or problem perspective, parents avoid the unwelcomed news of self-growth. For example, the therapist did not tell Mrs. Vasquez (of Chapter 4) that her own anxiety and depression was the cause of her daughter's anxiety. Such a message would be difficult to deliver. It would come with the embedded goal that she has to "get over it for her daughter to improve," thus, possibly contributing to her feelings of shame. Constructing activities that make both happier, however, helps Mrs. Vasquez become a coping model for how she would like Yolanda to think, feel, and behave in response to a trauma. Mutual growth in happiness becomes the goal.

Asking parents to become coping models for their children allows us to make them home-based therapists. Many parents easily accept this role. Asking parents to become coping models gives parents a chance to learn new skills for dealing with the issues mirrored in their children. In the process of helping their child, parents grow. Establishing family goals that lead to benefits across the entire family is a difficult skill, but it is one that makes use of the dense interactions that occur within a family and the particular roles members are willing to assume toward each other.

Research findings clearly support that happy, expressive parents are invaluable to their children. Happy parents promote children's prosocial development and mental health (Denham & Grout, 1992; Eisenberg, Fabes, & Spinrad, 2006). Even in adolescent children, parental emotion influences the parent-child relationship and the adolescent's adjustment (Bronstein, Briones, Brooks, & Cowan, 1996; Cook, Kenny, & Goldstein, 1991; Flannery, Montemayor, Eberly, & Torquati, 1993).

Helping parents understand their contributions to their children's growth can be perceived as a burden or a gift, pressure or an invitation. The goal of being a happier person is more easily accepted than a goal having to do with reducing a negative behavior. One common, but unfortunate, family behavior is the frequent expression of anger. Eisenberg and colleagues (1992) found that anger at home was related to anxiety at school and lower sympathy for other children. When negative emotions are displayed at home, helping children understand the cause can moderate the effects of parental anger (Denham & Grout, 1992). Also, Valiente and colleagues (2004) found that some negative affect at home may help children recognize the emotions in their peer group more accurately and be compassionate toward their peers. Family goals that include parental coping models and increases in happiness are likely to have positive effects on the family system even when none of the members perform the agreed-upon activities perfectly.

TERMINATION

The decision to terminate therapy is a process involving both the family members' and the therapist's appraisal of important aspects of readiness. The family members usually focus upon feeling confident that they know how to continue their growth or that enough growth occurred. Family members, especially the parental leadership, must have learned to listen to each person's expression of his or her quality of life if therapeutic processes are to continue without the therapist. The process of termination can be one of helping the family understand the importance of self-monitoring and self-disclosing of both positive and negative feelings. Recognizing negative emotions as a warning sign rather than a call to action requires discipline and compassion. Discussing negative feelings in the context of compassion is valuable for the family. The compassionate discussions involve understanding that negative feelings signal that something needs to change. Negative feelings should not be denied or regarded as bad, but the link between negative thought and negative action must be disrupted before the family terminates therapy (e.g., I can feel angry and talk about it, not hit).

Before terminating, families must also have learned to value positive feelings. This may seem like a very easy threshold to reach, but learning to pay attention to positive feelings is a challenge for many family members. When members can respond to each other's strengths and good news (i.e., *capitalization*), it is an indicator of each person's ability to grow and thrive. The family must understand that prolonged periods without positive feelings or with insufficient positive feelings is a signal for psychological danger. Chronic negative feelings cause intellectual, social, biological, and psychological harm. When a family knows how to create positive feelings without the therapist, they are ready for termination. Underscoring that positive feelings act as a change producer rather than simply a change indicator presents an important distinction in the appreciation of positive feelings (Fitzpatrick & Stalikas, 2008).

The door to return to future family therapy should be left wide open. During termination of the example family, Todd voiced a concern, "I hope dad won't go back to the way he was before." Todd's sentiment echoes the wishes of many clients we have served. Family strategies that result in positive change may still be effortful despite the good outcomes. Families may need inoculating statements that warn them that they may think they can revert to old patterns, because everything is going so well, but that would be a mistake. Maintaining efforts that support positive change requires persistent action.

We hope family members will not need family therapy because of additional trauma; however, we want them to feel free to return to work for further growth. Just as Tiger Woods still adjusted his golf swing while he was the best golfer in the world, we could be the most moral, happiest, energetic people, and still we could improve.

Suggesting that our clients could return to therapy to learn ways to make their lives better is not typical. We used to say, "I am ambivalent about seeing y'all again. I enjoy working with you so I would really enjoy seeing you again. However, if you come back I know it means that you hit a roadblock. I know roadblocks happen from time to time but I do not wish you to have a roadblock!"

Now the statement can be less ambivalent. Families can be encouraged to return to therapy—even with no roadblocks in sight. The positive psychology revolution will be complete when family therapy is thought of for growth as often as it is for problem resolution.

FUTURE

We look forward to case studies and large-scale research investigation of many variants of Positive Family Therapy. Positive Family Therapy will benefit from the development of more interventions that foster creative, compassionate growth. Positive Family Therapy opens the door to viewing therapy through a different lens. In the past, engaging in family therapy meant admitting family failure in the marital relationship and/or in helping a child develop. The stigma of seeking help for pathology meant accepting a family identity of deficiency. Avoiding or postponing family therapy is easy to understand when it is linked to shame and failure. We hope a new view of family therapy results in families receiving help sooner and increases the involvement of ethnic groups that historically under-utilize therapy.

Positive Family Therapy, however, means developing a family's ability to use all of its assets. Positive Family Therapy advances family determined values that are inclusive of each member. Engaging in Positive Family Therapy means a commitment to family excellence. Seeking Positive Family Therapy is a sign that a child is nurtured and a marital relationship is being enhanced.

References

Abraham, R. (2005). Emotional intelligence in the workplace: A review and synthesis. In R. Schulze & R. D. Roberts (Eds.), *Emotional intelligence: An international handbook* (pp. 255–270). Ashland, OH: Hogrefe & Huber.

Adams, G. A., King, L. A., & King, D. W. (1996). Relationships of job and family involvement, family social support, and work-family conflict with job and life satisfaction. *Journal of Applied Psychology, 81*(4), 411–420.

Adams, J. F., Piercy, F. P., & Jurich, J. A. (1991). Effects of solution focused therapy's "formula first session task" on compliance and outcome in family therapy. *Journal of Marital & Family Therapy, 17*(3), 277–290.

Adelman, H. S., & Taylor, L. (2000). Promoting mental health in schools in the midst of school reform. *Journal of School Health, 70*, 171–178.

Anderson, H. D. (1997). *Conversation, language, and possibilities.* New York: Basic Books.

Anderson, H. D., & Goolishian, H. (1988). Human systems as linguistic systems: Preliminary and evolving ideas about the implications for clinical theory. *Family Process, 27*, 371–393.

Argyle, M., & Martin, M. (1991). The psychological causes of happiness. In F. Strack, M. Argyle, & N. Schwarz (Eds.), *Subjective well-being: An interdisciplinary perspective* (pp. 77–100). Elmsford, NY: Pergamon Press.

Bandura, A. (1973). *Aggression: A social learning analysis.* Oxford, England: Prentice-Hall.

Barber, B. K. (1997). Adolescent socialization in context: The role of connection, regulation, and autonomy in the family. *Journal of Adolescent Research, 12*, 5–11.

Barber, B. K., Stolz, H. E., & Olsen, J. A. (2005). Parental support, psychological control, and behavioral control: Assessing relevance across time, culture, and method. *Monographs of the Society for Research in Child Development, 70*(4), 1–137.

Barber, B. K., Stolz, H. E., Olsen, J. E., & Maughan, S. L. (2004). Parental support, psychological control and behavioral control: Assessing relevance across time, method and culture. Manuscript submitted for publication.

Barnard, W. M. (2004). Parent involvement in elementary school and educational attainment. *Children and Youth Services Review, 26*, 39–62.

Bartlett, J. C., Burleson, G., & Santrock, J. W. (1982). Emotional mood and memory in young children. *Journal of Experimental Child Psychology, 34*, 59–76.

Bartlett, M. Y., & DeSteno, D. (2006). Gratitude and prosocial behavior: Helping when it costs you. *Psychological Science, 17*, 319–325.

Bateson, G. (1972). *Steps to an ecology of mind*. New York: Ballantine.

Bateson, G. (1974). *Double bind*. In S. Brand (Ed.), *II cybernetic frontiers* (pp. 9–33). New York: Random House.

Beach, S. R. H., & Tesser, A. (1995). Self-esteem and the extended self-evaluation maintenance model: The self in social context. In M. H. Kernis (Ed.), *Efficacy, agency, and self-esteem*. (pp. 145–170). New York: Plenum Press.

Bean, R. A., Barber, B. K., & Crane, D. R. (2006). Parental support, behavioral control, and psychological control among African American youth: The relationships to academic grades, delinquency, and depression. *Journal of Family Issues, 27*(10), 1335–1355.

Bean, R. A., Bush, K. R., McKenry, P. C., & Wilson, S. M. (2003). The impact of parental support, behavioral control, and psychological control on the academic achievement and self esteem of African American and European American adolescents. *Journal of Adolescent Research, 18*, 523–541.

Beck, A. T. (1976). *Cognitive therapy and the emotional disorders*. Oxford, England: International Universities Press.

Becvar, D. S., & Becvar, R. J. (2003). *Family therapy: A systemic integration*, (5th ed.) Boston: Allyn & Bacon.

Berg, I. K. (1994). *Family-based services: A solution-focused approach*. New York: Norton.

Berg, I. K. (1997). *Irreconcilable Differences. NTSC Video*. New York: Norton.

Berg, I. K., & de Shazer, S. (1993). Making numbers talk: Language in therapy. In S. Friedman (Ed.), *The new language of change: Constructive collaboration in psychotherapy* (pp. 5–24). New York: Guilford.

Berg, I. K., & Miller, S. D. (1992). *Working with the problem drinker: A solution-focused approach*. New York: Norton.

Billings, A. (1979). Conflict resolution in distressed and nondistressed married couples. *Journal of Consulting and Clinical Psychology, 47*(2), 368–376.

Bomar, J. A., & Sabatelli, R. M. (1996). Family system dynamics, gender, and psychosocial maturity in late adolescence. *Journal of Adolescent Research, 11*, 421–439.

Boscolo, L., Cecchin, G., Hoffman, L., & Penn, P. (1987). *Milan systemic family therapy: Conversations in theory and practice*. New York: Basic Books.

Bossard, J. H. S., & Boll, E. S. (1950). *Ritual in family living: A contemporary study*. Philadelphia: University of Pennsylvania Press.

Boyatzis, R. E., Goleman, D., & Rhee, K. S. (2000). Clustering competence in emotional intelligence: Insights from the emotional competence inventory. In R. Bar-On, & J. D. A. Parker (Eds.), *The handbook of emotional intelligence: Theory, development, assessment, and application at home, school, and in the workplace* (pp. 343–362). San Francisco: Jossey-Bass.

Bradford, K., Barber, B. K., Olsen, J. A., Maughan, S. L., Erickson, L. D., Ward, D., et al. (2003). A multi-national study of interparental conflict, parenting, and adolescent functioning: South Africa, Bangladesh, China, India, Bosnia,

Germany, Palestine, Colombia, and the United States. *Marriage and Family Review, 35*, 107–137.

Brickman, P., Coates, D., & Janoff-Bulman, R. (1978). Lottery winners and accident victims: Is happiness relative? *Journal of Personality and Social Psychology, 36*(8), 917–927.

Bronfenbrenner, U. (1999). Environments in developmental perspective: Theoretical and operational models. In S. L. Friedman & T. D. Wachs (Eds.), *Measuring environment across the life span: Emerging methods and concepts* (pp. 3–28). Washington, DC: American Psychological Association.

Bronstein, P., Briones, M., Brooks, T., & Cowan, B. (1996). Gender and family factors as predictors of late adolescent emotional expressiveness and adjustment: A longitudinal study. *Sex Roles, 34*(11–12), 739–765.

Bruner, J. (2004). The narrative creation of self. In L. E. Angus & J. McLeod (Eds.), *The handbook of narrative and psychotherapy: Practice, theory, and research* (pp. 3–14). Thousand Oaks, CA: Sage Publications.

Bryan, T., & Bryan, J. (1991). Positive mood and math performance. *Journal of Learning Disabilities, 24*, 490–494.

Bugental, D. B., Lin, E. K., & Susskind, J. E. (1995). Influences of affect on cognitive processes at different ages: Why the change? In N. Eisenberg (Ed.), *Social development. Review of personality and social psychology* (Vol. 15, pp. 159–184). Thousand Oaks, CA: Sage Publications.

Calame, R., and Parker, K. (2003). Reclaiming youth and families with "Family ART." *Reclaiming Children and Youth, 12*(3), 154–157.

Carey, J. R., Clicque, S. H., Leighton, B. A., & Milton, F. (1976). Test of positive reinforcement of customers. *Journal of Marketing, 40*, 98–100.

Carlson, C., & Christenson, S. L. (Eds.). (2005). Evidence based parent and family interventions in school psychology [Special issue]. *School Psychology Quarterly, 20*(4).

Carlson, D., & Perrewe, P. (1999). The role of social support in the stressor-strain relationship: An examination of work-family conflict. *Journal of Management, 25*, 513–540.

Carnevale, P., & Isen, A. M. (1986). The influence of positive affect and visual access on the discovery of integrative solutions in bilateral negotiation. *Organizational Behavior and Human Decision Processes, 37*, 1–13.

Carver, C. S. (2004). Negative affects deriving from the behavioral approach system. *Emotion, 4*, 3–22.

Cecchin, G. (1987). Hypothesizing, circularity, and neutrality revisited: An invitation to curiosity. *Family Process, 26*(4), 405–413.

Chao, R. K. (1994). Beyond parental control and authoritarian parenting style: Understanding Chinese parenting through cultural notion of training. *Child Development, 65*, 1111–1119.

Chao, R. K. (2001). Extending research on the consequences of parenting style for Chinese Americans and European Americans. *Child Development, 72*(6), 1832–1843.

Christenson, S. L. (2003). The family-school partnership: An opportunity to promote the learning competence of all students. *School Psychology Quarterly*, *18*(4), 454–482.

Cohen, S. (1988). Psychosocial models of the role of social support in the etiology of physical disease. *Health Psychology*, *7*, 269–297.

Cohen, S., Doyle, W. J., Skoner, D. P., Rabin, B. S., & Gwaltney, J. M. (1997). Social ties and susceptibility to the common cold. *Journal of the American Medical Association*, *277*, 1940–1944.

Cohn, M. A., Mehl, M. R., & Pennebaker, J. W. (2004). Linguistic markers of change psychological change surrounding September 11, 2001. *Psychological Science*, *15* (10), 687–693.

Conoley, C. W., Conoley, J. C, Ivey, D. C & Scheel, M. J. (1991). Enhancing consultation by matching the consultee's perspectives. *Journal of Counseling and Development*, *69*, 546–549.

Conoley, C. W., & Garber, R. A. (1985). Effects of reframing and self-control directives on loneliness, depression, and controllability. *Journal of Counseling Psychology*, *32*(1), 139–142.

Conoley, C. W., Graham, J. M., Neu, T., Craig, M. C., O'Pry, A., Cardin, S. A. (2003). Solution-focused family therapy with three aggressive and oppositional-acting children: An N = 1 empirical study. *Family Process*, *42*(3), 361–374.

Conoley, C. W., Padula, M. A., Payton, D. S., & Daniels, J. A. (1994). Predictors of client implementation of counselor recommendations: Match with problem, difficulty level, and building client strengths. *Journal of Counseling Psychology*, *41* (3-7.33), 124–130.

Coohey, C. (2001). The relationship between familism and child maltreatment in Latino and Anglo families. *Child Maltreatment*, *6*, 130–142.

Cook, W. L., Kenny, D. A., & Goldstein, M. J. (1991). Parental affective style risk and the family system: A social relations model analysis. *Journal of Abnormal Psychology*, *100*(4), 492–501.

Crean, H. F. (2008). Conflict in the latino parent-youth dyad: The role of emotional support from the opposite parent. *Journal of Family Psychology*, *22*(3), 484–493.

Cropanzano, R., & Wright, T. A. (1999). A 5-year study of change in the relationship between well-being and job performance. *Consulting Psychology Journal: Practice and Research*, *51*, 252–265.

Crowe, E., & Higgins, E. T. (1997). Regulatory focus and strategic inclinations: Promotion and prevention in decision-making. *Organizational Behavior and Human Decision Processes*, *69*, 117–132.

Dahl, R., Bathel, D., & Carreon, C. (2000). The use of solution-focused therapy with an elderly population. *Journal of Systemic Therapies*, *19*(4), 45–55.

Daus, C. S., & Ashkanasy, N. M. (2005). The case for the ability-based model of emotional intelligence in organizational behavior. *Journal of Organizational Behavior*, *26*(4), 453–466.

Davidson, E. S., & Smith, W. P. (1982). Imitation, social comparison, and self-reward. *Child Development*, *53*(4), 928–932.

Davidson, R. J., Kabat-Zinn, J., Schumacher, J., Rosenkranz, M., Muller, D., Santorelli, S. F., et al. (2003). Alternations in brain and immune function produced by mindfulness meditation. *Psychosomatic Medicine, 65,* 564–570.

Davis, B. P., & Knowles, E. S. (1999). A disrupt-then-reframe technique of social influence. *Journal of Personality and Social Psychology, 76*(2), 192–199.

De Jong, P., & Berg, I. K. (1998). *Interviewing for solutions.* Belmont, CA: Thomson Brooks/Cole Publishing Co.

de Shazer, S. (1982). *Patterns of brief family therapy.* New York: Guilford.

de Shazer, S. (1984). The death of resistance. *Family Process, 23,* 11–21.

de Shazer, S. (1985). *Keys to solution in brief therapy.* New York: Norton.

de Shazer, S. (1988). *Clues: Investigating solutions in brief therapy.* New York: Norton.

de Shazer, S., Dolan, Y., Korman, H., McCollum, E., Trepper, T., & Berg, I. K. (2007). *More than miracles: The state of the art of solution-focused brief therapy.* New York: Haworth Press.

Denham, S. A., & Grout, L. (1992). Mothers' emotional expressiveness and coping: Relations with preschoolers' social-emotional competence. *Genetic, Social, and General Psychology Monographs, 118*(1), 73–101.

Diener, E., & Oishi, S. (2005). The nonobvious social psychology of happiness. *Psychological Inquiry, 16*(4), 162–167.

Diener, E., Oishi, S., & Lucas, R. E. (2003). Culture, personality, and well-being. *Annual Review of Psychology, 54,* 403–425.

Diener, E., Sandvik, E. & Pavot, W. (1991) Happiness is the frequency, not the intensity, of positive versus negative affect. In F. Strack, M. Argyle, & N. Schwarz (Eds.), *Subjective well-being: an interdisciplinary perspective* (pp. 119–139). Oxford: Pergamon Press.

Duncan, S. W., Todd, C. M., Perlmutter, M., & Masters, J. C. (1985). Affect and memory in young children. *Motivation & Emotion, 9,* 391–405.

Durlak, J. A. (1995). *School-based prevention programs for children and adolescents.* Thousand Oaks, CA: Sage Publications.

Dweck, C. S. (1999). *Self-theories: Their role in motivation, personality, and development. Essays in social psychology.* New York: Psychology Press.

Eccles, J. S. (1997). User-friendly science and mathematics: Can it interest girls and minorities in breaking through the middle school wall? In D. Johnson (Ed.), *Minorities and girls in school: Effects on achievement and performance* (pp. 65–104). Thousand Oaks, CA: Sage Publications.

Eccles, J. S., Early, D., Frasier, K., Belansky, E., & McCarthy, K. (1997). The relation of connection, regulation, and support for autonomy to adolescents' functioning. *Journal of Adolescent Research, 12,* 263–286.

Eid, M., & Diener, E. (2001). Norms for experiencing emotions in different cultures: Inter- and intranational differences. *Journal of Personality and Social Psychology, 81*(5), 869–885.

Eisenberg, M. E., Olson, R. E., Neumark-Sztainer, D., Story, M., & Bearinger, L. H. (2004, August). *Correlations between family meals and psychosocial well-being among adolescents.* Archives of Pediatrics and Adolescent Medicine, 158, Downloaded from www.archpediatrics.com on October 2, 2008.

Eisenberg, N., Champion, C., & Ma, Y. (2004). Emotion-related regulation: An emerging construct. *Merrill-Palmer Quarterly: Special Issue: The Maturing of the Human Developmental Sciences: Appraising Past, Present, and Prospective Agendas, 50*(3), 236–259.

Eisenberg, N., Fabes, R. A., Carlo, G., & Karbon, M. (1992). Emotional responsivity to others: Behavioral correlates and socialization antecedents. In N. Eisenberg & R. A. Fabes (Eds.), *Emotion, self-regulation, and social competence, Feb 1991, Tempe, AZ* (pp. 57–73). San Francisco: Jossey-Bass.

Eisenberg, N., Fabes, R. A., Guthrie, I. K., & Reiser, M. (2000). Dispositional emotionality and regulation: Their role in predicting quality of social functioning. *Journal of Personality and Social Psychology, 78*(1), 136–157.

Eisenberg, N., Fabes, R. A., & Spinrad, T. L. (2006). Prosocial development. In N. Eisenberg, W. Damon & R. M. Lerner (Eds.), *Handbook of child psychology: Vol. 3, social, emotional, and personality development* (6th ed.). (pp. 646–718). Hoboken, NJ: John Wiley & Sons, Inc.

Eisenberg, N., Smith, C. L., Sadovsky, A., & Spinrad, T. L. (2004). Effortful control: Relations with emotion regulation, adjustment, and socialization in childhood. In R. F. Baumeister & K. D. Vohs (Eds.), *Handbook of self-regulation: Research, theory, and applications* (pp. 259–282). New York: Guilford.

Elliot, A. J., & Church, M.A. (2002). Client-articulated avoidance goals in the therapy context. *Journal of Counseling Psychology, 49*(2), 243–254.

Elliot, A. J., McGregor, H. A., & Gable, S. (1999). Achievement goals, study strategies, and exam performance: A meditational analysis. *Journal of Educational Psychology, 91,* 549–563.

Emmons, R. A., & McCullough, M. E. (2003). Counting blessings versus burdens: An experimental investigation of gratitude and subjective well-being in daily life. *Journal of Personality and Social Psychology, 84,* 377–389.

Emmons, R. A. & Shelton, C. M. (2002). Gratitude and the science of postive psychology. In C. R. Snyder & S. J. Lopez (Eds.), *Handbook of positive psychology* (pp. 459–471). Oxford: Oxford University Press.

Erchul, W. P., & Sheridan, S. M. (Eds.). (2008). *Handbook of research in school consultation: Empirical foundations for the field.* New York: Erlbaum.

Evans, S. W., Sapia, J. L., Axelrod, J., & Glomb, N. K. (2002). Practical issues in school mental health: Referral procedures, Negotiating special education, and confidentiality. In H. Ghuman, M. D. Weist, & R. Sarles (Eds.), *Providing mental health services to youth where they are: School- and community-based approaches* (pp. 75–94). New York: Brunner-Routledge.

Fensalson, K., & Beehr, T. (1994). Social support and occupational stress: Effects of talking to others. *Journal of Organizational Behavior, 14,* 157–175.

Fiese, B. H. (1993). Family rituals in alcoholic and nonalcoholic households: Relation to adolescent health symptomatology and problem drinking. *Family Relations, 42,* 187–192.

Fiese, B. H., Hooker, K. A., Kotary, L., & Schwagler, J. (1993). Family rituals in the early stages of parenthood. *Journal of Marriage and the Family, 55*, 633–642.

Fiese, B. H., Tomcho, T. J., Douglas, M., Josephs, K., Poltrock, S., & Baker, T. (2002). A review of 50 years of research on naturally occurring family routines and rituals: Cause for celebration? *Journal of Family Psychology, 16*(4), 381–390.

Fisch, R., Weakland, J. H., & Segal, L. (1982). *The tactics of change: Doing therapy briefly*. San Fransico, CA: Jossey-Bass.

Fitzpatrick, M. R., & Stalikas, A. (2008). Integrating positive emotions into theory, research, and practice: A new challenge for psychotherapy. *Journal of Psychotherapy Integration, 18*(2), 248–258.

Flannery, D. J., Montemayor, R., Eberly, M., & Torquati, J. (1993). Unraveling the ties that bind: Affective expression and perceived conflict in parent-adolescent interactions. *Journal of Social and Personal Relationships, 10*(4), 495–509.

Forgas, J. P., Burnham, D. K., & Trimboli, C. (1988). Mood, memory, and social judgments in children. *Journal of Personality and Social Psychology, 54*, 697–703.

Frank, J. D., & Frank, J. (2004). *Therapeutic components shared by all psychotherapies*. New York: Springer.

Franken, A. (1992). *I'm good enough, I'm smart enough, and doggone it, people like me!: Daily affirmations by Stuart Smalley Really*. New York: Dell.

Fraser, J. S., & Solovey, A. D. (2006) *Second-order change in psychotherapy: The golden thread that unifies effective treatments*. Washington, DC: American Psychological Association

Fredrickson, B. L. (1998). What good are positive emotions? *Review of General Psychology, 2*, 300–319.

Fredrickson, B. L. (2001). The role of positive emotions in positive psychology—the broaden-and-build theory of positive emotions. *American Psychologist, 56*, 218–226.

Fredrickson, B. L., & Branigan, C. (2005). Positive emotions broaden the scope of attention and thought-action repertoires. *Cognition & Emotion, 19*(3), 313–332.

Fredrickson, B. L., Tugade, M. M., Waugh, C. E., & Larkin, G. R. (2003). What good are positive emotions in crises? A prospective study of resilience and emotions following the terrorist attacks on the United States on September 11, 2001. *Journal of Personality and Social Psychology, 84*, 365–376.

Friedman, R. S., & Forster, J. (2001). The effects of promotion and prevention cues on creativity. *Journal of Personality and Social Psychology, 81*, 1001–1013.

Frijda, N. H., & Mesquita, B. (1994). The social roles and functions of emotions. In S. Kitayama & H. R. Markus (Eds.), *Emotion and culture: Empirical studies of mutual influence* (pp. 51–87). Washington, DC: American Psychological Association.

Froh, J. J., Sefick, W. J., & Emmons, R. A. (2008). Counting blessings in early adolescents: An experimental study of gratitude and subjective well-being. *Journal of School Psychology, 46*(2), 213–233.

Fromm, E. (1962). *The art of loving*. New York: Harper & Row.

Gable, S. L. (2008). Approach and avoidance motivation in close relationships. In J. P. Forgas, & J. Fitness (Eds.), Sydney symposium of social psychology, Sydney, NSW, Australia (pp. 219–234). New York: Psychology Press.

Gable, S. L., & Haidt, J. (2005). What (and why) is positive psychology? *Review of General Psychology, 9*, 103–110.

Gable, S. L., Reis, H. T., Impett, E. A., & Asher, E. R. (2004). What do you do when things go right? The intrapersonal and interpersonal benefits of sharing good events. *Journal of Personality and Social Psychology, 87*, 228–245.

Gallagher, M. W. (2008). Broadening the role of positive emotions within hope theory: A meta-analytic review. Paper at the annual convention of the American Psychological Association in Boston, MA.

Garbacz, S. A., Woods, K. E., Swanger-Gagne, M. S., Taylor, A. M., Black, K. A., & Sheridan, S. M. (in press). Conjoint behavioral consultation: The effectiveness of a partnership centered approach. *School Psychology Quarterly.*

Garber, J., Robinson, N. S., & Valentiner, D. (1997). The relations between parenting and adolescent depression: Self-worth as a mediator. *Journal of Adolescent Research, 12*, 12–33.

Gavazzi, S. M., Goettler, D. E., Solomon, S. P., & McKenry, P. C. (1994). The impact of family and peer differentiation levels on adolescent psychosocial development and problemmatic behaviors. *Contemporary Family Therapy, 16*, 431–448.

Gavazzi, S. M., & Sabatelli, R. M. (1990). Family system dynamics, the individuation process, and psychosocial development. *Journal of Adolescent Research, 5*, 499–518.

Gergen, K. J. (1985). The social constructionist movement in modern psychology. *American Psychologist, 40*(3), 266–275.

Gergen, K. J. (1997). The place of the psyche in a constructed world. *Theory & Psychology, 7*(6), 723–746.

Gergen, K. J. (2000). The coming of creative confluence in therapeutic practice. *Psychotherapy: Theory, Research, Practice, Training, 37*(4), 364–369.

Goetz, P. W., Robinson, M. D., & Meier, B. P. (2008). Attentional training of the appetitive motivation system: Effects on sensation seeking preferences and reward-based behavior. *Motivation and Emotion, 32*(2), 120–126.

Goldstein, A. P. (1999). *The prepare curriculum: Teaching prosocial competencies.* Champaign, IL: Research Press.

Goldstein, A. P., & Glick, B. (1989). *Aggression replacement training: A comprehensive intervention for aggressive youth.* Champaign, IL: Research Press.

Goldstein, A. P., Nensén, R., Daleflod, B., and Kalt, M. (2004). *New perspectives on aggression replacement training: Practice, research and application.* New York: Wiley.

Goleman, D. (1995). *Emotional intelligence.* New York: Bantam Books.

Gonzales, N. A., Deardorff, J., Formoso, D., Barr, A., & Barrera, M., Jr. (2006). Family mediators of the relation between acculturation and adolescent mental health. *Family Relations, 55*(3), 318–330.

Gottman, J. M. (1976). Behavior exchange theory and marital decision making. *Journal of Personality and Social Psychology, 34*(1), 14–23.

Gottman, J. M. (1979). *Marital interaction: Experimental investigations*. New York: Academic.

Gottman, J. M. (1994) *What predicts divorce?* Hillsdale, NJ: Lawrence Erlbaum Associates.

Gottman, J. M., & Levenson, R. W. (1999). What predicts change in marital interaction over time? A study of alternative medicine. *Family Process, 38*, 143–158.

Gottman, J. M., Markman, H., & Notarius, C. (1977). The topography of marital conflict: A sequential analysis of verbal and nonverbal behavior. *Journal of Marriage & the Family, 39*(3), 461–477.

Graczyk, P. A., Domitrovich, C. E., & Zins, J. E. (2003). Facilitating the implementation of evidence-based prevention and mental health promotion efforts in schools. In M. D. Weist, S. W. Evans, & N. A. Lever (Eds.), *Handbook of school mental health: Advancing practice and research* (pp. 301–318). New York: Kluwer Academic/Plenum Publishers.

Gray, M. R., & Steinberg, L. (1999). Unpacking authoritative parenting: Reassessing a multidimensional construct. *Journal of Marriage and Family, 61*, 574–587.

Greenberg, L. S., & Goldman, R. N. (2008). *Emotion-focused couples therapy: The dynamics of emotion, love, and power*. Washington, DC: American Psychological Association.

Greenberg, M. T., Weissberg, R. P., O'Brien, M. U., Zins, J. E., Fredericks, L., Resnik, H., et al. (2003). Enhancing school-based prevention and youth development through coordinated social, emotional, and academic learning. *American Psychologist: Special Issue: Prevention that Works for Children and Youth, 58* (6–7), 466–474.

Gushue, G. V., Greenan, D. E., & Brazaitis, S. J. (2005). Using the multicultural guidelines in couples and family counseling. In M. G. Constantine & D. W. Sue (Eds.), *Strategies for building multicultural competence in mental health and educational settings* (pp. 56–72). Hoboken, NJ: Wiley.

Hahlweg, K., Revenstorf, D., & Schindler, L. (1984). Effects of behavioral marital therapy on couples' communication and problem-solving skills. *Journal of Consulting and Clinical Psychology, 52*(4), 553–566.

Hare-Mustin, R. T. (1994). Dicourses in the mirrored room: A postmodern analysis of therapy. *Family Process, 33*, 19–35.

Haviland, J. M., & Lelwica, M. (1987). The induced affect response: Ten-week-old infants' responses to three emotion expressions. *Developmental Psychology, 23*, 97–104.

Herman, M. R., Dornbusch, S. M., Herron, M. C., & Herting, J. R. (1997). The influence of family regulation, connection, and psychological autonomy on six measures of adolescent functioning. *Journal of Adolescent Research, 12*, 34–67.

Higgins, T. E., Shah, J., & Friedman, R. (1997). Emotional responses to goal attainment: Strength of regulatory focus as moderator. *Journal of Personality and Social Psychology, 72*, 515–525.

Hill, N. E., Castellino, D. R., Lansford, J. E., Nowlin, P., Dodge, K. A., Bates, J. E., et al. (2004). Parent academic involvement as related to school behavior, achievement, and aspirations: Demographic variations across adolescence. *Child Development, 75,* 1491–1509.

Hoagwood, K. E. (2005). Family-based services in children's mental health: A research review and synthesis. *Journal of Child Psychology and Psychiatry, 46*(7), 690–713.

Hoffman, L. (1995). *Exchanging voices: A collaborative approach to family therapy.* London: Karnac.

Hollon, S. D., & Beck, A. T. (2004). Cognitive and congnitive-behavioral therapies. In M. J. Lambert (Ed.), *Garfield and Bergin's handbook of psychotherapy and behavior change: An empirical analysis* (5th ed., pp. 447–492). New York: Wiley.

House, J. S., Landis, K. R., & Umberson, D. (1988). Social relationships and health. *Science, 241,* 540–545.

Imber-Black, E., Roberts, J., & Whiting, R. (Eds.). (1988). *Ritual in families and family therapy.* New York: Norton.

Impett, E. A., Strachman, A., Finkel, E. J., & Gable, S. L. (2008). Maintaining sexual desire in intimate relationships: The importance of approach goals. *Journal of Personality and Social Psychology, 94*(5), 808–823.

Isen, A. M. (1999). Positive affect. In T. Dalgleish & M. J. Power (Eds.), *Handbook of cognition and emotion* (pp. 521–539). Chichester, England: Wiley.

Isen, A. M., Horn, N., & Rosenhan, D. L. (1973). Effects of success and failure on children's generosity. *Journal of Personality and Social Psychology, 27,* 239–247.

Jacobson, N. S., Follette, W. C., & McDonald, D. W. (1982). Reactivity to positive and negative behavior in distressed and nondistressed married couples. *Journal of Consulting and Clinical Psychology, 50*(5), 706–714.

Jensen, P. & Hoagwood, K. (Eds.). (2008). *Improving children's mental health through parent empowerment: A guide to assisting families.* New York, NY: Oxford University Press.

Jeynes, W. H. (2005). A meta-analysis of the relation of parental involvement to urban elementary school student academic achievement. *Urban Education, 40,* 237–269.

Johnston, T. B., Levis, M., & L'Abate, L. (1986). Treatment of depression in a couple with systematic homework assignments. *Journal of Psychotherapy & the Family.* Special Issue: Depression in the Family, 2(3–4), 117–128.

Kashdan, T. B., & Roberts, J. E. (2004). Trait and state curiosity in the genesis of intimacy: Differentiation from related constructs. *Journal of Social and Clinical Psychology, 23,* 792–816.

Kazdin, A. E. (1973). Covert Modeling and the Reduction of Avoidance Behavior. *Journal of Abnormal Psychology, 81*(1), 87–95.

Kazdin, A. E. (1981). Acceptability of child treatment techniques: The influence of treatment efficacy. *Behavior Therapy, 12,* 493–506.

Keeney, B. P. (1983). *Aesthetics of change.* New York: Guilford.

Keltner, D., & Kring, A. (1998). Emotion, social function, and psychopathology. *Review of General Psychology, 2,* 320–342.

Kenrick, D. T., Baumann, D. J., & Cialdini, R. B. (1979). A step in the socialization of altruism as hedonism: Effects of negative mood on children's generosity under public and private conditions. *Journal of Personality and Social Psychology, 37*, 747–755.

Kim, E., & Cain, K. C. (2008). Korean American adolescent depression and parenting. *Journal of Child and Adolescent Psychiatric Nursing, 21*(2), 105–115. doi:10.1111/j.1744–6171.2008.00137.x

Kim, S., Brody, G. H., & Murry, V. M. (2003). Longitudinal links between contextual risks, parenting, and youth outcomes in rural African American families. *Journal of Black Psychology, 29*, 359–377.

Koole, S. L., Smeets, K., vanKnippenberg, A., & Dijksterhuis, A. (1999). The cessation of rumination through self-affirmation. *Journal of Personality and Social Psychology, 77*, 111–125.

Kratochwill, T. R. (2007). Preparing psychologists for evidence-based practice: Lessons learned and challenges ahead. *American Psychologist, 62*, 826–843.

Kratochwill, T. R., Albers, C. A., & Shernoff, E. S. (2004). School-based interventions. *Child and adolescent psychiatric clinics of North America, 13*, 885–903.

Lakey, B., McCabe, K. M., Fisicaro, S. A., & Drew, J. B. (1996). Environmental and personal determinants of support perceptions: Three generalizability studies. *Journal of Personality and Social Psychology, 70*, 1270–1280.

Lane, J., & Anderson, N. H. (1976). Integration of intention and outcome in moral judgment. *Memory & Cognition, 4*, 1–5.

Langston, C. A. (1994). Capitalizing on and coping with daily-life events: Expressive responses to positive events. *Journal of Personality and Social Psychology, 67*, 1112–1125.

Lench, H. C., & Levine, L. J. (2008). Goals and responses to failure: Knowing when to hold them and when to fold them. *Motivation and Emotion, 32*, 127–140.

Lerner, H. (1985). *The dance of anger: A woman's guide to changing the patterns of intimate relations.* New York: Harper & Row.

Lerner, H. (1989). *The dance of intimacy: A woman's guide to courageous acts of change in key relationships.* New York: Harper & Row.

Linehan, M. M. (1993). *Cognitive behavioral treatment of Borderline Personality Disorder.* New York: Guilford.

Lyubomirsky, S. (2008). *The how of happiness: A scientific approach to getting the life you want.* New York: Penguin.

Lyubomirsky, S., King, L., & Diener, E. (2005). The benefits of frequent positive affect: Does happiness lead to success? *Psychological Bulletin, 131*, 803–855.

Lyubomirsky, S., Sheldon, K. M., & Schkade, D. (2005). Pursuing happiness: The architecture of sustainable change. *Review of General Psychology, 9*, 111–131.

Mammen, O., Kolko, D., & Pilkonis, P. (2003). Parental cognitions and satisfaction: Relationship to aggressive parental behavior in child physical abuse. *Child Maltreatment, 8*, 288–301.

Margolin, G., & Wampold, B. E. (1981). Sequential analysis of conflict and accord in distressed and nondistressed marital partners. *Journal of Consulting and Clinical Psychology, 49*(4), 554–567.

Markson, S., & Fiese, B. H. (2000). Family rituals as a protective factor for children with asthma. *Journal of Pediatric Psychology, 25*(7), 471–479. Retrieved from www.csa.com.

Maruyama, M (1963). The second cybernetics: Deviation-amplifying mutual causal processes. *American Scientist, 5,* 164–179.

Mason, C. A., Cauce, A. M., Gonzales, N., & Hiraga, Y. (1996). Neither too sweet nor too sour: Problem peers, maternal control, and problem behavior in African American adolescents. *Child Development, 67,* 2115–2130.

Maturana, H. (1974). Cognitive strategies. In H. von Foerster (Ed.), *Cybernetics of cybernetics* (pp. 457–469). Urbana: University of Illinois.

Mayer, J. D., Salovey, P., & Caruso, D. (2000). Models of emotional intelligence. In R. J. Sternberg (Ed.), *Handbook of intelligence* (pp. 396–420). New York: Cambridge University Press.

Mayer, J. P., & Davidson, W. S., II. (2000). Dissemination of innovation as social change. In J. Rappaport & E. Seidman (Eds.), *Handbook of community psychology* (pp. 421–443). Dordrecht, Netherlands: Kluwer Academic Publishers.

McCullough, M. E., Emmons, R. A., & Tsang, J. A. (2002). The grateful disposition: A conceptual and empirical topography. *Journal of Personality and Social Psychology, 82,* 112–127.

McCullough, M. E., Kilpatrick, S. D., Emmons, R. A., & Larson, D. B. (2001). Is gratitude a moral affect? *Psychological Bulletin, 127,* 249–266.

McCullough, M. E., & Snyder, C. R. (2000). Classical sources of human strength. *Journal of Social and Clinical Psychology, 19*(1), 1–10.

McCullough, M. E., Tsang, J.-A., & Emmons, R. A. (2004). Gratitude in intermediate affective terrain: Links of grateful moods to individual differences and daily emotional experience. *Journal of Personality and Social Psychology, 86,* 295–309.

McGinnis, E., & Goldstein, A. P. (1990). *Skill-streaming in early childhood: Teaching prosocial skills to the preschool and kindergarten child.* Champaign, IL: Research Press.

McNamee, S., & Gergen, K. J. (Eds.). (1992). *Therapy as social construction.* London: Sage.

Medora, N., Wilson, S., & Larson, J. J. (2001). Attitudes toward parenting strategies, potential for child abuse, and parental satisfaction of ethnically diverse low-income U.S. mothers. *Journal of Social Psychology, 141,* 335–348.

Meichenbaum, D. H. (1971). Examination of model characteristics in reducing avoidance behavior. *Journal of Personality and Social Psychology, 17,* 298–307.

Minuchin, S. (1974). *Families and family therapy.* Cambridge: Harvard University Press.

Moss, M. S., & Moss, S. Z. (1988). Reunion between elderly parents and their distant children. *American Behavioral Scientist: Special Issue: Rituals and Reunions, 31*(6), 654–668.

Mounts, N. S. (2004). Contributions of parenting and campus climate to freshmen adjustment in a multiethnic sample. *Journal of Adolescent Research, 19,* 468–491.

Myers, D. G. (1992). *The pursuit of happiness: Who is happy and why.* New York: William Morrow.

National Institute of Mental Health (2001). *Blueprint for change: Research on child and adolescent mental health.* A report of the National Advisory Mental Health Council's Workgroup on Child and Adolescent Mental Health Intervention and Deployment. (NIH Publication No. 01–4985, p. 93). Rockville, MD: Author.

Nezlek, J. B., & Gable, S. L. (2001). Depression as a moderator of relationships between positive daily events and day-to-day psychological adjustment. *Personality and Social Psychology Bulletin, 27*(12), 1692–1704.

Oishi, S. (2002). The experiencing and remembering of well-being: A cross-cultural analysis. *Personality and Social Psychology Bulletin, 28,* 1398–1406.

Okamoto, S., & Robinson, W. P. (1997). Determinants of gratitude expressions in England. *Journal of Language and Social Psychology, 16,* 411–433.

O'Neill, R. E., Horner, R. H., Albin, R. A., Storey, J., & Sprague, J. (1997). *Functional analysis: A practical guide* (2nd ed.). Pacific Grove, CA: Brooks Cole.

Osterberg, L., & Blaschke, T. (2005). Adherence to medication. *New England Journal of Medicine, 353*(5), 487–497.

Padula, M. A., Conoley, C. W., & Garbin, C. P. (1998). The dimensions underlying loneliness counseling interventions: A multidimensional scaling solution. *Journal of Counseling & Development, 76*(4), 442–451.

Parasuraman, S., Greenhaus, J. H., & Granrose, C. S. (1992). Role stressors, social support, and well-being among two-career couples. *Journal of Organizational Behavior, 13*(4), 339–356.

Parasuraman, S., Purhoit, Y., Godshalk, V., & Beutell, N. (1996). Work and family variables, entrepreneurial career success, and psychological well being. *Journal of Vocational Behavior, 48,* 275–300.

Park, N., Peterson, C., & Seligman, M. E. P. (2006). Character strengths in fifty-four nations and the fifty US states. *The Journal of Positive Psychology, 1*(3), 118–129.

Patterson, G. R. (1982). *Coercive family processes.* Eugene, OR: Castalia.

Penn, P. (1982). Circular questioning. *Family Process, 21*(3), 267–280.

Penn, P. (1985). Feed-forward: Future questions, future maps. *Family Process, 24*(3), 299–310.

Pennebaker, J. W. (1997). *Opening up: The healing power of expressing emotion.* New York: Guilford.

Peterson, C., Seligman, M. E. P., Yurko, K. H., Martin, L. R., & Friedman, H. S. (1998). Catastrophizing and untimely death. *Psychological Science, 9,* 127–130.

Pullis, M. (1992). An analysis of the occupational stress of teachers of the behaviorally disordered: Sources, effects and strategies for coping. *Behavioral Disorders, 17*(3), 191–201.

Raush, H. L., Barry, W. A., Hertel, R. K., & Swain, M. A. (1974). *Communication conflict and marriage.* Oxford, England: Jossey-Bass.

Reddy, L. A., & Goldstein, A. P. (2001). Aggression replacement training: A multimodal intervention for aggressive adolescents. Residential Treatment for Children & Youth. Special Issue: Innovative Mental Health Interventions for Children: Programs that Work, *18*(3), 47–62.

Rind, B., & Bordia, P. (1995). Effect of servers thank-you and personalization on restaurant tipping. *Journal of Applied Social Psychology, 25*, 745–751.

Robbins, M. S., Alexander, J. F., Newell, R. M., & Turner, C. W. (1996). The immediate effect of reframing on client attitude in family therapy. *Journal of Family Psychology, 10*(1), 28–34.

Rogers, C. R. (1957). The necessary and sufficient conditions of therapeuitic personality change. *Journal of Consulting Psychology, 21*, 95–103.

Rones, M., & Hoagwood, K. (2000). School-based mental health services: A research review. *Clinical Child & Family Psychology Review, 3*(4), 223–241.

Rosenfield, S. & Berninger, V. (2009). *Implementing Evidence–Based Academic–Based Interventions in School Settings.* New York: Oxford University Press.

Ruch, W. (1993). Exhilaration and humor. In M. Lewis & J. M. Haviland (Eds.), *Handbook of emotions* (pp. 605–616). New York: Guilford.

Rudes, J., & Guterman, J. T. (2007). The value of social constructionism for the counseling profession: A reply to hansen. *Journal of Counseling & Development, 85*(4), 387–392.

Safdar, S., Lay, C., & Struthers, W. (2003). The process of acculturation and basic goals: Testing a multidimensional individual difference acculturation model with Iranian immigrants in Canada. *Applied Psychology: An International Review, 52*(4), 555–579.

Salovey, P., Rothman, A. J., Detweiler, J. B., & Steward, W. T. (2000). Emotional states and physical health. *American Psychologist, 55*, 110–121.

Sapolsky, R. M. (2004). *Why zebras don't get ulcers* (3rd ed.). New York: Macmillan.

Sarason, I. G. (1973). Test anxiety and cognitive modeling. *Journal of Personality and Social Psychology, 28*, 58–61.

Schaap, C. (1984). Conflicthantering en huwelijkssatisfactie. Conflict resolution and marital satisfaction. *Nederlands Tijdschrift Voor De Psychologie En Haar Grensgebieden, 39*(7), 396–403.

Schaefer, E. S. (1965). A configurational analysis of children's reports of parental behavior. *Journal of Consulting Psychology, 29*, 552–557.

Scheel, M. J. (1994). Circular questioning and neutrality: An empirical investigation of the process. (ProQuest Information & Learning). Dissertation Abstracts International: Section B: The Sciences and Engineering, 54 (7-B) Retrieved from www.csa.com.

Scheel, M. J., & Conoley, C. W. (1998). Circular questioning and neutrality: An investigation of the process relationship. *Contemporary Family Therapy: An International Journal, 20*(2), 221–235.

Scheel, M. J., Hanson, W. E., & Razzhavaikina, T. I. (2004). The process of recommending homework in psychotherapy: A review of therapist delivery methods, client acceptability, and factors that affect compliance. *Psychotherapy: Theory, Research, Practice, Training, 41*(1), 38–55.

Schmidt, N., & Woolaway-Bickel, K. (2000) The effects of treatment compliance on outcome in cognitive-behavioral therapy for Panic Disorder: Quality versus quantity. *Journal of Consulting and Clinical Psychology, 68*(1), 13–18.

Schoenwald, S. K., Henggeler, S. W., Brondino, M. J., & Rowland, M. D. (2000). Multisystemic Therapy: Monitoring Treatment Fidelity. *Family Process, 39*(1), 83–103.

Schunk, D. H., & Hanson, A. R. (1985). Peer models: Influence on children's self-efficacy and achievement. *Journal of Educational Psychology, 77*(3), 313–322.

Seligman, M. E. P., & Csikszentmihalyi, M. (2000). Positive psychology: An introduction. *American Psychologist, 55*(1), 5–14.

Seligman, M. E. P., Steen, T. A., Park, N., & Peterson, C. (2005). Positive psychology progress: Empirical validation of interventions. *American Psychologist, 60*(5), 410–421.

Selvini-Palazzoli, M., Boscolo, L., Cecchin, G. F., & Prata, G. (1977). Family rituals: A powerful tool in family therapy. *Family Process, 16*(4), 445–453.

Sheldon, K. M., & King, L. (2001). Why positive psychology is necessary. *American Psychologist, 56*(3), 216–217.

Sheridan, S. M., & Burt, J. B. (in press). Family-centered positive psychology. In C. R. Synder & S. J. Lopez (Eds.), *Handbook of positive psychology* (2nd ed.). New York: Oxford University Press.

Sheridan, S. M., Clarke, B. L., & Burt, J. D. (2008). Conjoint behavioral consultation: What do we know and what do we need to know? In W. P. Erchul & S. M. Sheridan (Eds.), *Handbook of research in school consultation: Empirical foundations for the field* (pp. 171–202). Mahwah, NJ: Lawrence Erlbaum.

Sheridan, S. M., & Kratochwill, T. R. (2008). *Conjoint behavioral consultation: Promoting family-school connections and interventions*. New York: Springer.

Sluzki, C. E., & Beavin, J. (1965). Simetría y complementaridad: Una definición operacional y una tipología de parejas. Symmetry and complementarity: An operational definition and typology of dyads. *Acta Psiquiátrica y Psicológica De America Latina, 11*(4), 321–330.

Smith, S., Ingoldsby, B. B., Miller, J. E., & Hamon, R. R. (Eds.). (2008). *Exploring family theories*. Oxford, England: Oxford University Press.

Snyder, C. R. (1994). *The psychology of hope: You can get there from here*. New York: Free Press.

Snyder, C. R. (2002). Hope theory: Rainbows in the mind. *Psychological Inquiry, 13*, 249–275.

Snyder, C. R., Lapointe, A. B., Crowson, J. J., Jr., & Early, S. (1998). Preferences of high- and low-hope people for self-referential input. *Cognition and Emotion, 12*, 807–823.

Staw, B. M., Sutton, R. I., & Pelled, L. H. (1994). Employee positive emotion and favorable outcomes at the workplace. *Organization Science, 5*, 51–71.

Steinberg, L., Dornbusch, S. M., & Brown, B. B. (1992). Ethnic differences in adolescent achievement: An ecological perspective. *American Psychologist, 47*, 723–729.

Steinberg, L., Mounts, N. S., Lamborn, S. D., & Dornbusch, S. M. (1991). Authoritative parenting and adolescent adjustment across varied ecological niches. *Journal of Research on Adolescence, 1*(1), 19–36.

Stuart, R. B. (1980). *Helping couples change: A social learning approach to marital therapy.* New York: Guilford.

Sugai, G., Horner, R. H., Dunlap, G., Hieneman, M., Lewis, T., Nelson, C. M., et al. (2000). Applying positive behavior support and functional behavioral assessment in schools. *Journal of Positive Behavior Interventions, 3,* 131–143.

Sutherland, O. (2007). Therapist positioning and power in discursive therapies: A comparative analysis. *Contemporary Family Therapy: An International Journal, 29* (4), 193–209.

Taylor, S. E. (2003). *Health psychology.* New York: McGraw-Hill.

Tesser, A., Gatewood, G., & Driver, M. (1968). Some determinants of gratitude. *Journal of Personality and Social Psychology, 9,* 233–236.

Tesser, A., Millar, M., & Moore, J. (1988). Some affective consequences of social comparison and reflection processes: The pain and pleasure of being close. *Journal of Personality and Social Psychology, 54*(1), 49–61.

Thibaut, J. W., & Kelley, H. H. (1959). *The social psychology of groups.* New York: Wiley.

Thomas, M., & Choi, J. B. (2006). Acculturative stress and social support among Korean and Indian immigrant adolescents in the United States. *Journal of Sociology & Social Welfare, 33*(2), 123–143.

Tomkins, S. S. (1962). *Affect, imagery, and consciousness: Vol. I. The positive affects.* New York: Springer.

Tomm, K. (1987a). Interventive interviewing: I. Strategizing as a fourth guideline for the therapist. *Family Process, 26*(1), 3–13.

Tomm, K. (1987b). Interventive interviewing: II. Reflexive questioning as a means to enable self-healing. *Family Process, 26*(2), 167–183.

Tomm, K. (1988). Interventive interviewing: III. Intending to ask lineal, circular, strategic, or reflexive questions? *Family Process, 27*(1), 1–15.

Tov, W., & Diener, E. (2007). Culture and subjective well-being. In S. Kitayama, & D. Cohen (Eds.), *Handbook of cultural psychology.* (pp. 691–713). New York: Guilford Press.

Trinidad, D. R., Unger, J. B., Chou, C., & Johnson, C. A. (2004). The protective association of emotional intelligence with psychosocial smoking risk factors for adolescents. *Personality and Individual Differences, 36*(4), 945–954.

Troll, L. E. (1988). New thoughts on old families. *The Gerontologist, 28*(5), 586–591.

Tronick, E. Z. (1989). Emotions and emotional communication in infants. *American Psychologist: Special Issue: Children and Their Development: Knowledge Base, Research Agenda, and Social Policy Application, 44*(2), 112–119.

Tsang, J. (2006). Gratitude and prosocial behaviour: An experimental test of gratitude. *Cognition & Emotion, 20,* 138–148.

Uchino, B. N., Cacioppo, J. T., & Kiecold-Glazer, J. K. (1996). The relationship between social support and physiological processes: A review with emphasis on underlying mechanisms and implications for health. *Psychological Bulletin, 119,* 488–531.

U.S. Public Health Service (2000). *Report on the Surgeon General's Conference on Children's Mental Health: A national action agenda.* Washington, DC: U.S. Government Printing Office.

Valiente, C., Eisenberg, N., Shepard, S. A., Fabes, R. A., Cumberland, A. J., Losoya, S. H., et al. (2004). The relations of mothers' negative expressivity to children's experience and expression of negative emotion. *Journal of Applied Developmental Psychology, 25*(2), 215–235.

Videon, T. M., & Manning, C. K. (2003). Influences on adolescent eating patterns: The importance of family meals. *Journal of the American Dietetic Association, 32,* 365–373.

von Bertalanffy, L. (1976). *General system theory: Foundations, development, applications* (rev. ed.). New York: George Braziller.

Watkins, P. C. (2004). Gratitude and subjective well-being. In R. A. Emmons, & M. E. McCullough (Eds.), *The psychology of gratitude.* (pp. 167–192). New York: Oxford University Press.

Watzlawick, P., Weakland, J. H., & Fisch, R. (1974). *Change: Principles of problem formation and problem resolution.* Oxford, England: Norton.

Weare, K. (2000). *Promoting mental, emotional and social health: A whole school approach.* London: Routledge.

Weeks, G. R., & L'Abate, L. (1979). A compilation of paradoxical methods. *American Journal of Family Therapy, 7*(4), 61–76.

Weiner, B., Russell, D., & Lerman, D. (1978). Affective consequences of causal ascriptions. In J. H. Harvey, W. J. Ickes, & R. F. Kidd (Eds.), *New directions in attribution research* (vol. 2, pp. 59–90). Hillsdale, NJ: Erlbaum.

Weiner, B., Russell, D., & Lerman, D. (1979). The cognition—emotion process in achievement and related contexts. *Journal of Personality and Social Psychology, 37,* 1211–1220.

Weiss, L. H., & Schwartz, J. C. (1996). The relationship between parenting types and older adolescents'personality, academic achievement, adjustment, and substance use. *Child Development, 67,* 2101–2114.

Weisz, J. (2004). *Psychotherapy for children and adolescents: Evidence-based treatments and case examples.* New York: Cambridge University Press.

Wender, P. H. (1968). Vicious and virtuous circles: The role of deviation amplifying feedback in the origin and perpetuation of behavior. *Psychiatry: Journal for the Study of Interpersonal Processes, 31*(4), 309–324.

White, J. M., & Klein, D. M. (2007). *Family theories* (3rd ed.). Thousand Oaks, CA: Sage Publications.

White, M. & Epston, D. (1990). Narrative means to therapeutic ends. New York: W. W. Norton.

Wills, T. A., Sandy, J. M., Shinar, O., & Yaeger, A. (1999). Contributions of positive and negative affect to adolescent substance use: Test of a bidimensional model in a longitudinal study. *Psychology of Addictive Behaviors, 13,* 327–338.

Wilson, W. (1967). Correlates of avowed happiness. *Psychological Bulletin, 67*, 294–306.

Witt, J. C., & Elliott, S. N. (1982). The response cost lottery: A time efficient and effective classroom intervention. *School Psychology Review, 20*, 155–161.

Wolf, M. M. (1978). Social validity: The case for subjective measurement or how applied behavior analysis is finding its heart. *Journal of Applied Behavior Analysis, 11*(2), 203–214.

Wolin, S. J., & Bennett, L. A. (1984). Family rituals. *Family Process, 23*, 401–420.

Wolin, S. J., Bennett, L. M., & Noonan, D. L. (1979). Family rituals and the recurrence of alcoholism over generations. *American Journal of Psychiatry, 136*, 589–593.

Wolin, S. J., Bennett, L. A., Noonan, D. L., & Teitelbaum, M. A. (1980). Disrupted family rituals: A factor in the generational transmission of alcoholism. *Journal of Studies of Alcohol, 41*, 199–214.

Wolpe, Joseph. (1990). *The practice of behavior therapy.* Tarrytown, NY: Pergamon Press.

Wood, A., Joseph, S., & Linley, A. (2007). Gratitude — parent of all virtues. *The Psychologist, 20*(1), 18–21.

Wood, A. M., Joseph, S., & Linley, P. A. (2007). Coping style as a psychological resource of grateful people. *Journal of Social and Clinical Psychology, 26*, 1108–1125.

Wood, A. M., Joseph, S., & Maltby, J. (2008). Gratitude uniquely predicts satisfaction with life: Incremental validity above the domains and facets of the five factor model. *Personality and Individual Differences, 45*(1), 49–54. doi:10.

Wood, A. M., Maltby, J., Stewart, N., Linley, P. A., & Joseph, S. (2008). A social-cognitive model of trait and state levels of gratitude. *Emotion, 8*(2), 281–290.

Wright, T. A., & Staw, B. M. (1999). Affect and favorable work outcomes: Two longitudinal tests of the happy-productive worker thesis. *Journal of Organizational Behavior, 20*, 1–23.

Yeh, C. J., & Inose, M. (2003). International students' reported English fluency, social support satisfaction, and social connectedness as predictors of acculturative stress. *Counselling Psychology Quarterly, 16*(1), 15–28.

Yoon, E., Lee, R. M., & Goh, M. (2008). Acculturation, social connectedness, and subjective well-being. *Cultural Diversity and Ethnic Minority Psychology, 14*(3), 246–255.

Zautra, A. J., Schultz, A. S., & Reich, J. W. (2000). The role of everyday events in depressive symptoms for older adults. In G. M. Williamson, D. R. Shaffer & P. A. Parmelee (Eds.), *Physical illness and depression in older adults: A handbook of theory, research, and practice.* (pp. 65–91). Dordrecht, Netherlands: Kluwer Academic Publishers.

Zayas, L. H. (1992). Childrearing, social stress, and child abuse: Clinical considerations with Hispanic families. *Journal of Social Distress and the Homeless, 1*, 291–309.

Zimmerman, M. A., Ramirez-Valles, J., Zapert, K. M., & Maton, K. I. (2000). A longitudinal study of stress-buffering effects for urban African American male adolescent problem behaviors and mental health. *Journal of Community Psychology, 28,* 17–33.

Zins, J. E., Weissberg, R. P., Wang, M. C., & Walberg, H. J. (Eds.). (2004). *Building academic success on social and emotional learning: What does the research say?* New York: Teachers College Press.

AUTHOR INDEX

SUBJECT INDEX